FOR ALL

FOR ALL

Revolutionary Poets Brigade

Edited by
Kristina Brown
John Curl
Karen Melander-Magoon
Barbara Paschke

ISBN: 978-0-938392-18-7

Kallatumba Press
San Francisco, CA

http://revolutionarypoetsbrigade.org/
Printed in the United States of America.

CONTENTS

VISUAL ARTISTS

Front Cover: Bengt Berg, *photo*
Back Cover: Ayo Ayoola-Amale, *Bare Trees*
Cover Design: Kristina Brown

p. 17: Virginia Barrett
p. 37: Adrian Arias
p. 55: Satish Gupta
p. 64: Agneta Falk, *photo*; Kristina Brown, *chalk*
p. 69: Marco Cinque
p. 85: Cathleen Williams
p. 128: Andrena Zawinski
p. 153: Horst Tuuloskorpi

PRODUCTION

Proofreading: Barbara Paschke
Layout: John Curl

FOR ALL

PREFATORY

These poems and art works explore and celebrate what is at stake for all of us and what we can do together. Democracy is in danger all over the world. Every day communities and habitats are destroyed. Sexism, classism, and racism flourish. Democracy as we know it is not serving the needs of large numbers of people. The oligarchs, much smaller than 1%, make the key decisions and choose to create a world in which many people starve and many work ceaselessly, but cannot pay their bills. A planet where climate change continues to warm and weather goes wild. Wars, starvation, loss of habitat, mass migrations all result from actions of the oligarchs, but are left for other people to suffer. The ruling elite care only about power, tolerate the appearance of democracy as long as it does not threaten their power, and fund populist authoritarian politicians toward perpetuating those ends.

But a new generation has risen up to protest war and the slaughter of innocents. Poets, artists and all creative people can seize this opportunity to focus our powers toward creating a more just and enlightened world For All.

As artists we refuse to cede the future to the billionaires and dictators, to the power of capital and those who wield it. Poetry provides an essential voice to address the struggle to preserve democracy by standing together.

In this international anthology we showcase works by 87 poets and 10 artists, from 20 countries, in 10 languages, on the theme For All. On the cover we offer a red carnation to represent both resistance and community.

We ask that you walk thoughtfully through these pages and take whatever inspiration you may find.

"All for one and one for all." D'Artagnan.

Jack Hirschman presente!

Editors
Kristina Brown, John Curl,
Karen Melander-Magoon, Barbara Paschke

FOR ALL

AYO AYOOLA-AMALE *(Nigeria)*

BARE TREES

And then it happened-
one dumb morning, grave
In a crowded flimsy shack, ungraceful
A big storm ran into dirty, narrow streets
and alleys swarm through
like whaling vessels-
chewed children,
choke us like a rope looped about our necks,
and left dangling from heavy beams.
Neem trees are thin as a wire,
Palm trees are dry as bone, only drier
howling on the stone walls tilted like a ball shaking on the rim
a vein in our hearts walked out -
as soggy as paste, bulging out all around.
We threw away all that came into our hands
scratching like hens in the sand and gravel.
Gorges and streams up to the mountains
overran our fields, destroyed our cassava,
razed down our leaky huts.
In a steady stream, we sank into shallow water
like vessels that rotted away and sank at their moorings.
Plastics bite large chunks of rivers
draped with mouths, belching with foul smells from
panting fishes with pipes tied to their chin
Scraps cling to lungs
and lungs turn to dirt stuck
like a mule sucked
down into the mud, drowned.
Women with skeletal bodies and their babies sucking
milk less breast like bugs that clung to the roots
of tufts of lifeless grass.
The bombs inside the sun,
stiff bare trees froze in the cut

to death.
We know man, an ass,
with an axe
hacks off
polar bears,
elephants and break
yawning farmlands.
They set fire
on the cradle.
Everybody did so.

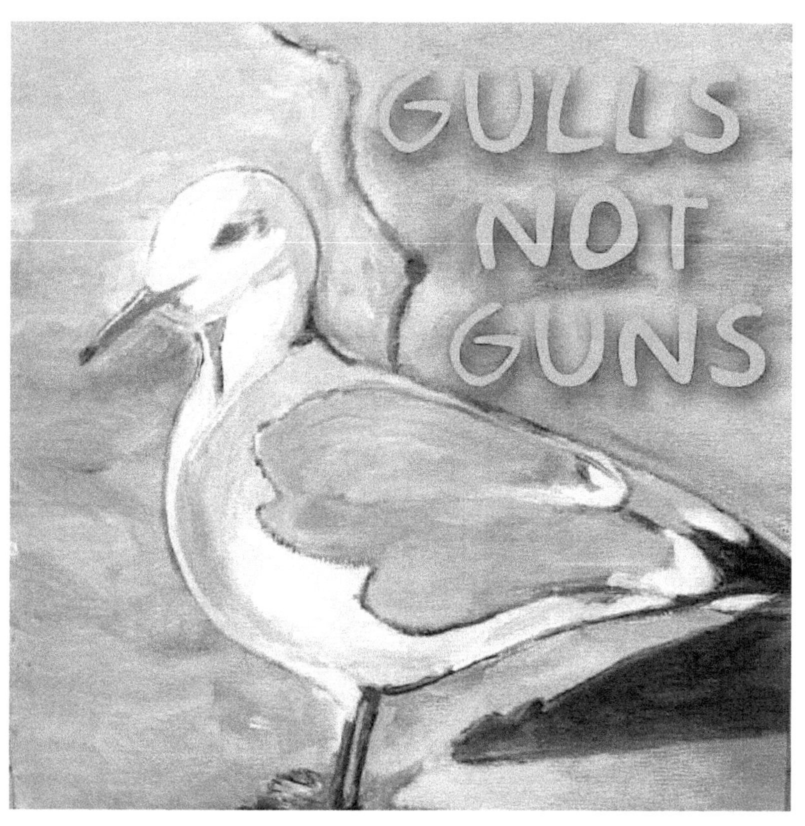

Virginia Barrett

ADRIAN ARIAS *(Peru/USA)*

VENUS ROTA

Soy la Venus de la destrucción,
mi rostro desmantelado en la oscuridad.
Mis músculos y nervios, carne viva,
no sé por dónde mirar, respirar, hablar

pues, ya no puedo hablar.

Cómo hallar la felicidad y belleza
cuando han caído 13,430 niños,
han bombardeado hospitales y hogares
han bombardeado mis sueños.

pues, ya no puedo soñar

Mi corazón estalla en pedazos,
sus trozos se pierden en el vacío, en el silencio de la tragedia,
en la melancolía del lamento.

Pues, ya ni me puedo lamentar.

Cada cuerpo que cae, mi cuerpo muere,
mis escombros se transforman en raíces,
en semillas muertas que emergen de la desolación
en la risa del payaso que solo saber dar miedo

Pues, ya ni miedo tengo.

Me convierto en el monstruo
de mi propia muerte,
en el eco de la destrucción y el dolor,
en la sombra que se alza sobre el horror

ADRIAN ARIAS *(Peru/USA)*

BROKEN VENUS

I am the Venus of destruction,
my face dismantled in the darkness.
My muscles and nerves, living flesh,
I don't know where to look, breathe, speak

Well, I can't talk anymore.

How to find happiness and beauty
when 13,430 children have fallen,
hospitals and homes have been bombed
They have bombarded my dreams.

Well, I can't dream anymore

My heart bursts into pieces,
its pieces are lost in the void,
in the silence of tragedy,
in the melancholy of lament.

Well, I can't even regret it anymore.

Every body that falls, my body dies,
my rubble becomes roots,
in dead seeds that emerge from desolation
in the clown's laughter that only knows how to be scary

Well, I'm not even afraid anymore.

I become the monster
of my own death,
in the echo of destruction and pain,
in the shadow that rises over the horror

Pues, soy la representación del horror

Pero aún en medio de la desesperación,
busco la luz en la noche más oscura,
el resplandor de la esperanza perdida,
la fuerza para renacer de las cenizas

Pues, al menos cenizas soy.

Well, I am the representation of horror

But even in the midst of despair,
I look for the light in the darkest night,
the glow of lost hope,
the strength to be reborn from the ashes

Well, at least I am ashes.

MAHNAZ BADIHIAN *(Iran/USA)*

HOW MANY MORE BROKEN WINGS CAN WE ENDURE?

The earth and sun are consistent everywhere,
and the moon is everyone's companion.
Yet humans are divided, separated, and unintelligent,
with love compartmentalized.

We fail to share our love with everyone,
unlike the moon, the sun, or the earth.
Our hearts are too small to hold love for all,
our appetite is too large, consuming others' food.
Our brains are limited, seeing only a fraction,
thinking of only a few, not all.

Our insatiable desires and sexuality
result in offspring by the minute,
many left without food, shelter, or love.

Now, we cling to Artificial Intelligence,
created by the unintelligent.
An AI programmed by selfish humans
may succumb to the magnificence of nature.

This new AI could be the dark path
towards further unintelligent, criminal ways of life.

LISBIT BAILEY

IT'S HUMAN

"The universe is made of stories, not of atoms."
Muriel Rukeyser

Humans exist in an infinite universe
in a milky way
in a galaxy
on one small sphere

It's human to put faith
in something larger than ourselves

Call it hope,
if faith smacks of organized religion

Or call it a search for meaning,
if hope feels too passive

We invent "isms" so far from the truth,
they've become facts
easier to believe in than even love

The universe evokes awe in its expansiveness
it's without the "isms" we've made up
to malign "them "and praise "us"

Mysteries, that don't need to be outwitted,
have become liabilities

In these mean times,
humans sprint toward annihilation

We're too busy to live our lives reverently
We're too busy trying to make ends meet

We've been set against each other
in this capitalist world that's growing in on itself

In this capitalist world that's already plundering
outer space for new feeding grounds

Already a field of our debris
Already private property to be bought and sold.

LYNNE BARNES

H.O.P.E.

Hold on, pain ends
said someone who turned
hope into an acronym.

Here at ground level,
swirly world, friends far-flung,
connection needs effort
as stresses tug.

Call friend in cognitive decline—
service as strap-to-the-mast binding
in this world's wild winds.

Friends fighting civil court battles,
friends losing mothers to
disease and depression.

Old pal trying to claw her way out of
past trauma's trap-net tangles—oh, how she
shone in her acting class yesterday.

I pull back, to a view from the moon—
yearn, for more heart, more art-felt creation
as the forces of demagoguery
threaten to swallow civilization.

Hey kids, maybe we *do* have to put on a show,
a Mickey Rooney/Judy Garland
extravaganza— aural, visual, visceral,
prolific with sky-flying fireworks of change
rising from somewhere-over-that-rainbow.

Auditions now for a globe theater show
of post-warstorm harmony. Red Alert,
dear fellow all-the-world's-a-stage players.
Unite, pump iron—let's lose our *them and us* fat-
headedness and wagging fingers, plump our
atrophying muscles of lovingkindness,
build up arms as strength for lifting others

until dopamine floods our public squares,
no needles required, soaking us all
in its mojo, drowning despair.

Hold on, pain ends
said someone who turned
hope into an acronym.

VIRGINIA BARRETT

THE ABILITY TO FLY

Gray seagulls lined up
like bankers in suits
along the jagged edge
of the old coastal road now
slipped into the sand.
Wings held tight at their sides
they stare out at the waves
as if trying to ascertain
if the market today
will bring a high yield.

But of course the gulls
know, in their collective
bird-souls, that the ocean
is a continuous flow
of give and take while
the bankers think
(for greed's greedy sake)
of only the latter—
                    of take and take.

What a difference
the ability to fly can make.

BENGT BERG *(Sweden)*

OM SKOR, VÄRLD OCH DRÖMMAR

Du är inte bara där dina skor är
utan också där dina drömmar gror ...

Det står ett par skor vid dörren
Det finns en värld utanför
– Vad väntar du på?

Om du inte går ut i världen
kommer den och hämtar dig

Du behöver skorna,
Världen behöver dig

Använd din röst varje dag,
inte bara vart fjärde år

Allt förändras, ingenting
Kommer i morgon att vara
som det är idag

Varje dag är ny,
Under gryningens ögonlock
finns de drömmar
som kan sätta vingar
på de slitnaste skor

Du har inte en chans - ta den!

BENGT BERG *(Sweden)*

ABOUT SHOES, WORLD AND DREAMS

(You're not just where your shoes are
but also where your dreams are growing ...)

There's a pair of shoes at the door
There's a world outside
– What are you waiting for?

If you don't go out into the world
It will come for you

You need the shoes,
The world needs you

Use your voice every day,
not just every four years

Everything changes, nothing
tomorrow will be
as it is today

Every day is new,
Under the eyelids of dawn
there are the dreams
that can set wings
on the most worn shoes

You don't have a chance – take it!

(Translated from Swedish by the author)

JUDITH AYN BERNHARD

SIGNS OF SPRING

As spring approaches
the air softens
streets fill with
people seeking
friendship and light

Hand in hand
their eyes open wide
lovers stand together
looking at each other
with joy and wonder

Fathers and sons
mothers and daughters
people with no
children at all laugh
at the antics of toddlers

These are the days of
hope and renewal
cruelty is left behind as
daffodils break open the
crumbled chilly dirt

And through an open
window you hear
Louis Armstrong
thinking to himself
What a Wonderful World

THE DESPICABLE

America was built on free labor being slaves
Lies, deceit, and winner take all
Corruption at its finest before Chicago was
It escalated to become Manifest Destiny / westward expansion, eminent domain
The issue of slavery has now created a stumbling block for this sin sick nation
And Westward Ho! Has caused the stench of this sickness to rise,
becoming smoke like fog on the falsified pages of history
Ask any Native American about a treaty
Winner take all is at the crap table, it's really capitalism on the loose
The slaves arrived in chains set free
There was never compensation for these freed people
Only brutality directed at them
So now because of the long term brutality and oppression
Many whites think that black people will seek revenge
It didn't happen, back then and not today
But a white woman in Texas doesn't want her son to learn about the horrors and atrocities
She would rather continue to exercise racial hatred based on ignorance

DANIEL BROOKS

THE PATH THAT LIES BEFORE US II

Don't forget to look up
To the sky and be one
With your limitations
Don't forget to look up
to no one but the people
and your community
your fellow human beings
Don't forget to look upon
the waters far and wide
reflecting sunshine
embodying the light

*

No individual
No hero
No shero
No savior
No saint
No church
No judge
No court
No politician
No celebrity
No mogul
No corporation
No nonprofit
No branch
No one
Will save us
Only the oppressed
The masses
Organized
And determined
Can liberate
Themselves

KRISTINA BROWN

IN GAZA

On the screen in front of me,

at our breakfast table,
as we eat
omelets and biscuits and green salad with
tomatoes,
and the rich smell of my parents' coffee rises into the
brisk morning air,

hundreds
of children
with bowls in their hands
crowd together.
With big eyes and hollow cheeks
They push and shove,
fight for food.
Their little arms are skinny sticks.
Most of them manage to have their bowls filled with
porridge,
But some of the smaller ones keep being pushed
aside.

The children are all bigger and older than I am.

I'm worried for all of them.

I look over at my mother.
"Where are their parents? Why aren't they feeding
them?"
My mother grits her teeth.
She doesn't want to tell me.

Horror swells in my chest.
My eyes widen.
I say, "The parents don't have food. Or have they taken all the moms and dads away to camps?"
My parents exchange glances.

I'm only almost four, but I know
One of my parents is about to tell me a hard truth.

My father licks his lips.
Oh no. This is going to be a bad one,
something I'll wish wasn't true.
Like all those people who were murdered
in WWI
and the Holocaust
and the colonization of the Americas.

He begins,
"Sometimes, people use food as a weapon
against everyone in a country.
But they don't want to be accused of murdering
children,
so they allow a little food in."

"You mean,
If all the adults don't or can't do what the people
blocking the food want,
everyone could starve to death?"
He nods.

I see a country with countless tables.
In every city and town and village,
regiments of tables are set with white tablecloths
and plates and cups, forks and knives and spoons.

But when the people sit down,
there is no food.
Everywhere children begin to cry, to wail they are
hungry.

The tables turn into legions of rectangular white
stones
cover miles of green hillside.

I say,
"Huge numbers of people could die
Like WWI but without the trenches and guns."

My father nods.

"Don't the killers know how wrong they are?
How will they ever live down killing all those people?"

My father's eyes burn. "They think the end justifies
the means."

I gasp. "They're evil! Something bad should happen
to them."

My father nods."Maybe. But be careful.
Don't become what you fight against."

So now,

I march against the genocide in Gaza.
I write another letter to a politician.

I write these words.

JANET CANNON

MY HIGH SCHOOL STUDENT

she forgets about melanin
sometimes treats me without
bias i saw her smile once
in class the one for at risk

futures to graduate with a
hope diploma that divorces
poverty for a better life a year
later as i'm rushing from my

day job to my night community
college teaching gig at the
building doorway she stops
me abruptly repeating my

name excitedly she blurts non-
stop *do you remember me from*
english class? i'm a student
here a community college

student because of you what
you said about how we can do
anything we try for... so happy
emphatically i say *good job*

we talk awhile before rushing to
our respective classes she with
her bright smile beaming huge like
a hug that won't let go like a moon

full of gratitude bigger than a sky
full of stars in her heart where
her dreams breathe where she
found her truth all by herself.

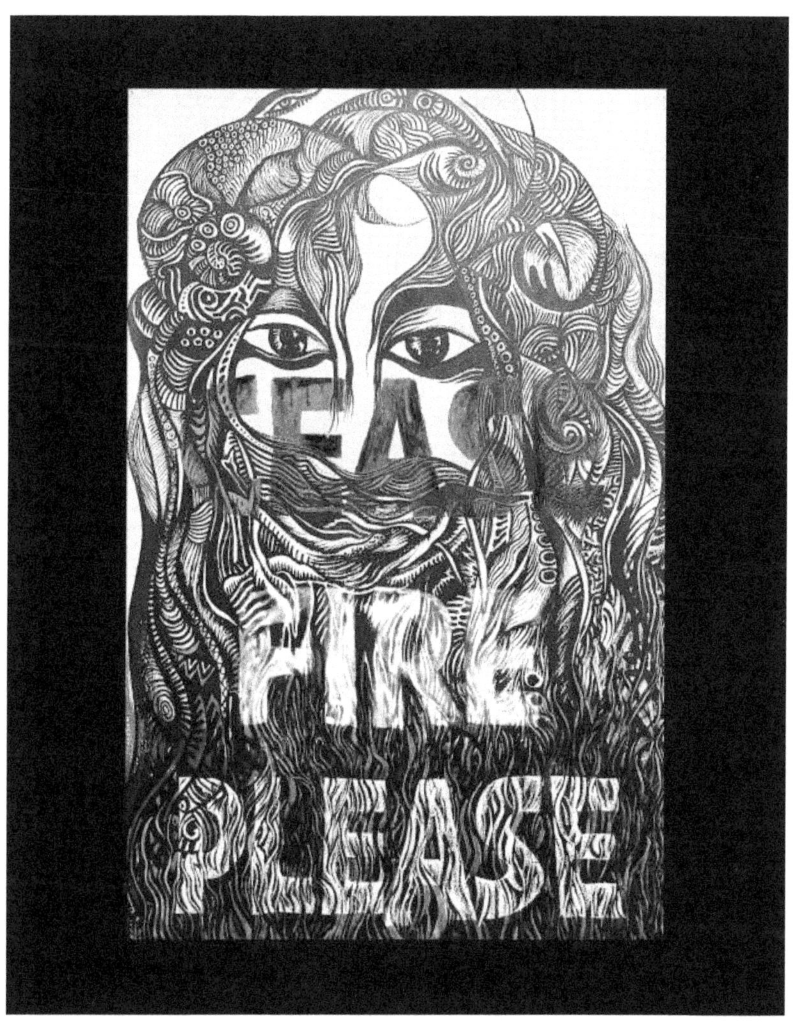

Adrian Arias

YOLANDA CATZALCO

CAN A POEM CHANGE THE COURSE OF HISTORY?

Can a poem change the course of history?
Can an artist paint the future?
Can a singer sing a song of unity?
Can a vision of the Planetariat governing
The world be seen
As the ultimate path of working people,
Gathering those who early 20th century
Communists labeled "lumpen proletariat"?
The homeless of today whose crime
In some cities such as New York City
Is panhandling?
Or to live in tents or on cardboards
On the cement,
If they're fortunate enough to sleep on,
Even in the rain?

Or to shoplift items from billion dollars
Profits conglomerates
In order so hungry, sockless vagrant
Shoplifters don't starve?

Can I go on?
Enumerating the cans of possibilities,
Of alternatives to this wretched, economic,
Political, capitalist system?
Where women are no longer allowed
Freedom of choice?
Where the before Roe vs. Wade, 1973 law,
Young women had no option than illegal,
Abortion clinics,
Where, many times, terror stories of
Illegal abortion surgery deaths were common?

Where there are fighters willing to fight
To end the never-called, terrorism,
Mind blowing deaths from starvation
Of 13,000 children in USA who died
Of hunger a year or more ago?

Where different religions can co-exist
Without fear of retaliation stemming from
Actions about their land being stolen
For the sake of a Prophecy?

Can we sleep at night knowing
Palestinians are being assassinated
For fighting for the right to return,
For the return of their land?

Where 80-year plus senior Holocaust
Survivor women in Ukraine & in Russia
Don't have enough to eat?

Can a poem change the course of history?

MARCO CINQUE *(Italy)*

all'odio
non cedere passo
che di forza ha bisogno
il perdono

§§§

sogno una resa dei conti
dove la rabbia degli ultimi
impari almeno una buona mira

§§§

il sangue preteso
dalla giustizia è rosso
come quello sparso
dall'ingiustizia

§§§

comprare
consumare
perderti
nell'inutilità
irrinunciabile

§§§

un altro mondo
è impossibile
se non cominci
dal tuo

MARCO CINQUE (Italy)

don't give way
to hate
since pardon
requires strength

§§§

I dream a showdown
where the rage of the last
will learn to have a sure aim at least

§§§

red is the blood
expected by justice
as that shed
by injustice

§§§

to buy
to consume
to lose oneself
in the obsolete
uselessness

§§§

another world
is impossible
unless you start
with your own

§§§

l'uguaglianza vive
nel rispetto del diverso
non nella tirannia degli uguali

§§§

se Dio diventasse donna
e tutti gli uomini, finalmente
la piantassero di sentirsi Dio
forse il mondo a venire
non dovrà più vergognarsi
del nostro essere umani
senza essere umani

§§§

tu, uomo di questo tempo
che non hai tempo da perdere
ma che ti stai perdendo

§§§

equality lives
in the respect of the different
not in the tyranny of the alike

§§§

if God were a woman
and all men would eventually
stop feeling like God
maybe the world to come
wouldn't be ashamed
of our being human
without being human

§§§

you, man of our time,
who have no time to lose
but who are losing yourself

(Translated from Italian by Alessandra Bava)

FRANCIS COMBES *(France)*

UN TOAST

Le soleil a mis la main à la pâte
et voici que le jour lève
blond et doré

Ne pas s'entretuer sur la terre des hommes
ce n'est pas assez

Viens, l'ami, assieds-toi à cette table
Partage le pain
Et le vin

Et portons, comme autrefois, un toast
à l'amitié des peuples

Il y a assez de la place
au soleil
pour nous tous.

FRANCIS COMBES *(France)*

TOAST

The sun has placed its hand on the dough
and here is the day rising
glazed and golden

Don't kill each other on the earth of men
It's not enough

Come, friend, sit at the table
Share the bread
And the wine

And raise, like other times, a toast
to the friendship of the people

There's enough room
in the sun
for all

(Translated from French by Barbara Paschke)

KITTY COSTELLO

TO MY ITALIAN AMERICAN BROTHERS AND SISTERS UPON THE TOPPLING OF COLUMBUS STATUES *

Have no fear.
Signups for Italian American heroes start here.
Smelt Frank Rizzo into Sacco & Vanzetti.
Smelt Columbus into Lawrence Ferlinghetti,
and while we're at it, cast Mario Andretti.

Praise George Moscone and Quentin Tarantino
Joe Di Maggio, Diane di Prima and Al Pacino,
or Madonna, Serpico and Caesar Cardini,
Nancy Pelosi, Dr. Fauci and Chef Boyardee.

The list has begun. Say their names out loud.
Keep adding to it until you feel proud.

** The City of San Francisco removed the statue of Columbus at Coit Tower on June 18, 2020.*

The City of Philadelphia removed the statue of former mayor and police chief Frank Rizzo on June 3, 2020.

ANITA ODENA CRUZ

WHAT IT'S LIKE TO LIVE THIS LONG

Decades past the immigrant
who strived at a new land filled

with hopes and aspirations for
the future and his children, hung

with pockets of car keys and coins
to teach them about hard work, thrift.

The day he retired, moved to Vegas
picked him up at Harry Reid airport.

During first visit- how hard, he said
the hours, the way he danced with bosses.

It is better this way, he said when he can
breathe easy every morning after listening to

clatter of shoes on the way to another
paycheck like numbers on the calendar.

I forgot how to savor a dream, he said,
as Vegas makes me live on fantasy's world

like rainbows above without rain. I'm
chasing another wheel of fortune when I

will have my turn, but now in house living
In death's time, questioning whether I

needed to win one, the television in front
all day long, telling me I lost the smell of

fresh air, excitement of seeing the children
get their diplomas, untarnished by neon lights.

ROMEO ALCALA CRUZ *(Philippines/USA)*

LIGHT IN THE SKY AT NIGHT. 1934.

Last night, green light in the sky. The
handwriting on the wall as war is about
to come. For the whole month, the swirling
green snake above ready to bite everybody
shaking their heads in fear. Poison. Death.
Overwhelming eyes, spreading reach over
the world. Have the heavens given up the
fight? The oracle in the wind streams, that
which we breathe, We live. We dream. We
hope for the best.

Last night it was all green lights as it embraced
peace for the last time. As darkness is about
to come sooner than later as jackboots resounded
over Vienna yesterday, The screams. The fear.
The terror. The damnation of saints. The destruction
of synagogues, churches. Yesterday, the madman
shrieked over the air waves as a python is ready
to swallow us whole.

Last night. The green light over the land, The
abolition of rights and love, The fortress coming like
a motionless train with millions to die on the way
To the chimneys. The camps like eagles sweeping
the night. Last night, the carving of angels and
coming out of gargoyles.

Last night the green light over the land, Even as
prophets slide and cower behind doors speechless.
The trials of the innocents in the halls of deceit. Fools
gorging on glutton of greed after the beer putsch of
Munich. And the terrible curse on the parade grounds,
last night, the Sabbath of murderers and monsters.
for the war will start soon.

Last night the green light over the land, the installation of bombers and submarines and tanks. The construction of killing machines. Last night, the sign of another inferno to come and the death of children. Last night, the handwriting of God on the wall.

Last night the green light over the land, The defeat that we can save Abel from Imminent death, the fall of paradise as our parents were banished from Eden. Last night the last prayer after sunset and the adoration of madmen to come. Last night was a terrible sign.

Last night, the green light over the land. As poets whisper with their pens, trying to exorcise the curse as Joseph lost his tongue, The Pharaoh in rampage after the Great Depression the land in hock to the pawnbrokers. Kill them All! Kill the slaves, where the Nile river open their wounds before the pyramids of gold and silver. Kill them all! On the crag by the leaning towers. O my revenge! O give me the dagger to begin now!

Last night, the green light over the land as the poor in their fireless lodgings dropped the headlines of evening papers: Anschluss, the madman has the right to expand his fangs and belt his long tail. The madman is at the operator of history and history will go to the hustler the murderer, the shock trooper!

Raise the drumroll of marching feet over the cobbled stones of the capitals of Europe before the madman's empire of the shark and the tiger establish death and killing machines. Surrender to his claws and jaws or rise as a dove to repudiate the lies and terrible destruction to descend.

JOHN CURL

BORDERS OF THE MIND

The boundary between
dandelion and rabbit
earthworm and soil
fish and water
seagull and wind
Ireland and Ulster
Juárez and El Paso
Gaza and Israel
Ukraine and Russia
every mother dries her eyes
while the birds fly over the borders.

The boundary between
wolf and wolf
lamb and lamb
wolf and lamb
stalker and stalked
victim and violator
everywhere the children cry
while the birds fly over the borders.

Daughters of Abraham
Arab sons of Semites,
Celtic cousins, sons of Slavs
daughters of the Rus
sons of the Americas
daughters of the world.
Today's maps are drawn
not by rivers, valleys, mountains,
native populations. Today's borders
are not defined by Nature's designs
but by power and imperial wars.
Everywhere the ghosts pass by
while the birds fly over the borders.

The people of the northern coast
the children of the eastern slope
A mountain divides two lands
a lake has opposite shores
a river two banks, a valley two sides
everywhere the wise women sigh
while the birds fly over the borders.

LUCILLE LANG DAY

TIME AND MONEY

Devlin, age five, says we should do away
        with time and money.
They interfere with our lives each day.
Devlin, age five, says we should do away
        with clocks and coins. Why not just play
when we want, let things be free?
Devlin, age five, says we should do away
        with time and money.

CAROL DENNEY

THIS IS THE GARDEN THAT STOPPED A WAR

key of G, concertina

put your head against the bark
of any tree in People's Park
they'll say what they're standing for
this is the garden that stopped a war
find a place to rest your head
plant a simple flower bed
all are welcome rich and poor
this is the garden that stopped a war

Chorus: this is the garden they tried to take
we are the people they tried to break
this is the landmark we're standing for
this is the garden that stopped a war

music dance and food to share
smiling people everywhere
sing together cry no more
this is the garden that stopped a war
wander through the sparkling grass
set your thoughts adrift at last
watch the clouds come back to shore
this is the garden that stopped a war

Chorus: this is the garden they tried to take
we are the people they tried to break
this is the landmark we're standing for
this is the garden that stopped a war

clouds that dance across the sky
waltz with birds that dip and fly

seagulls circle bow and soar
this is the garden that stopped a war
put your head against the bark
of any tree in People's Park
they'll say what they're standing for
this is the garden that stopped a war

Chorus: this is the garden they tried to take
we are the people they tried to break
this is the landmark we're standing for
this is the garden that stopped a war

"This Is the Garden That Stopped A War" is my way of sailing past the excuses people use for the current proposal to destroy people's park by replacing it with luxury student housing which one could build anywhere. Walking in the grass, leaning against a tree, listening to music - these are my responses. People's Park is, thanks to a handful of us who formed a nonprofit and filled out the application for federal landmark status, now on the National Register of Historic Places. People's Park, if you're listening, explains itself. ***Carol Denney, co-founder, People's Park Historic District Advocacy Group***

GERMAIN DROOGENBROODT *(Belgium)*

INDOCTRINATED INTELLIGENCE

The void
—stripped of all meaning—
has become mundane.

What one should think or do
is preprogrammed.

The image
which we see in the mirror
is no longer our own image.

***

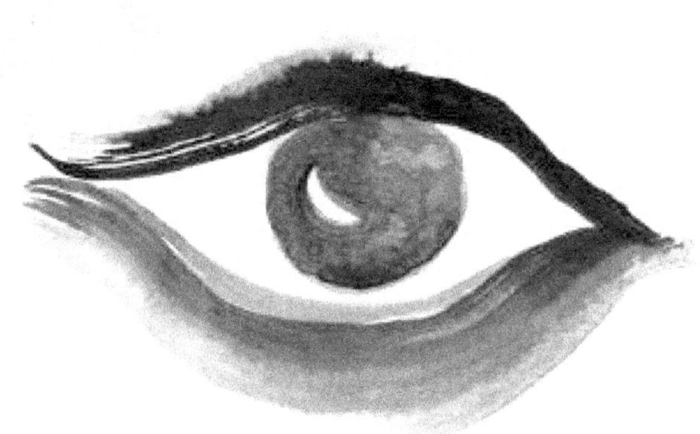

Painting by Satish Gupta

CARLOS RAÚL DUFFLAR

IN SOLIDARITY TO THE INDIGENOUS PEOPLE OF THE WORLD – Free Leonard Peltier Now & Saharawi Libre

in this forgotten corner of history
nothing is new beneath the Sun
over the past centuries
the Western world has plagued
Abya Yala – Latin America and the Caribbean
Turtle Island – US and Canada
and the world
and the transformation into colonialism of grief
under the Monroe Doctrine
the mark of blood
hunger
the robbing of the land
genocide
the weapon of oppression
the coronation of Colombo of Genoa
as a saint in the House of Capital
a monstrous heart with no light
of compassion and love
in their civilization of greed, of caste system,
apartheidism, warmongering, and vampirism
than embracing humanity and harmony to the universe
from their hidden mask of false liberal fascism
the propaganda of lies
about their past and their present
has become a graveyard of self-destruction on the Earth
let us lift our voice
for I am a volunteer Poet Laureate
for peace, solidarity, and friendship
where a new dawn will rise

in the spirit of the Diggers
a road into the future
Dr. Martin Luther King's saying:
"It is not possible to be in favor of justice for some people
and not be in favor of justice for all people"

MAURO FFORTISSIMO

YOU WANT TO KNOW ABOUT IMMIGRANTS

It is raining and very cold
and there they are
under awnings
by the gas station minimart
hovering like pigeons on a cornice

no work today
fields too wet
roofs slippery
lawn muddy for mowing
nothing to do at home
because home is just a mattress
laid on the floor of a damp garage
where to sleep with other guests...

and while you and I
sit warm and comfy drinking steaming coffee
preparing a yummy meal
complaining how slow the wi-fi is...
immigrants are somehow confident
of the work to come

you see, yours and my fences
that the wind blew down
leaky roofs
and the tree branches that fell
all will need repair
when these rains stop

so we'll drive to the closest
Home Depot for supplies

and get us a laborree or two
cheap daily wages
to put our house in order
and remove debris

but for now they hang
cold and wet as "wet backs"
those immigrants ruining our workforce
and draining our social services
with demands of healthcare
and paid vacations!

Yes, what a storm we just had...

DAVID FLEISCHMAN

TEN HAIKU MOTIF ON SUN

The Sun is our star
It's the key to complex life
Myths and facts abound

Facts about the Sun
Are known and then are not known
Who can say not I

The Sun rose each day
On the Garden of Eden
And all saw its glow

It sustained us then
It continues to this day
It's eternal, right?

The Sun's benefits
Are too many to mention
Light and warmth are two

It provides power
By helping plants to flourish
Plants are then consumed

The plants are basic
To the food chain that sustains
All life on the Earth

The warmth of the Sun
Promotes evaporation
And weather patterns

The Sun shines its light
On Earth through the atmosphere
Turning the sky blue

The Sun's energy
Creates power and much more
It creates beauty

MARCOS FREITAS *(Brazil)*

CARAVANÇARÁ

venho de milhares de eras de Sete Cidades
sou um milhão de civilizações gueguês
pinto com sangue os paredões de meus atos
        incompletos no Boqueirão da Pedra Furada
gravo na terra indecifráveis geoglifos
        em picos de morros da Serra das Confusões
renasço em arte naïf nas espinhas de peixes
        fósseis da Chapada do Araripe
enquanto na Serra Vermelha sobram apenas
        as cinzas da ignorante ganancia de alguns

MARCOS FREITAS *(Brazil)*

CARAVANSARY

i come from thousands of eras of Sete Cidades
i am a million of indigenous civilizations
i paint with blood the walls of my incomplete deeds.
        at Boqueirão da Pedra Furada
i record into the earth indecipherable geoglyphs
        in mountain peaks of Serra das Confusões
i rebirth in naive art on the fossil fish
        bones of Chapada do Araripe
while at Serra Vermelha only
        the ashes of the ignorant gain of some people remain

(Translated from Portuguese by the author)

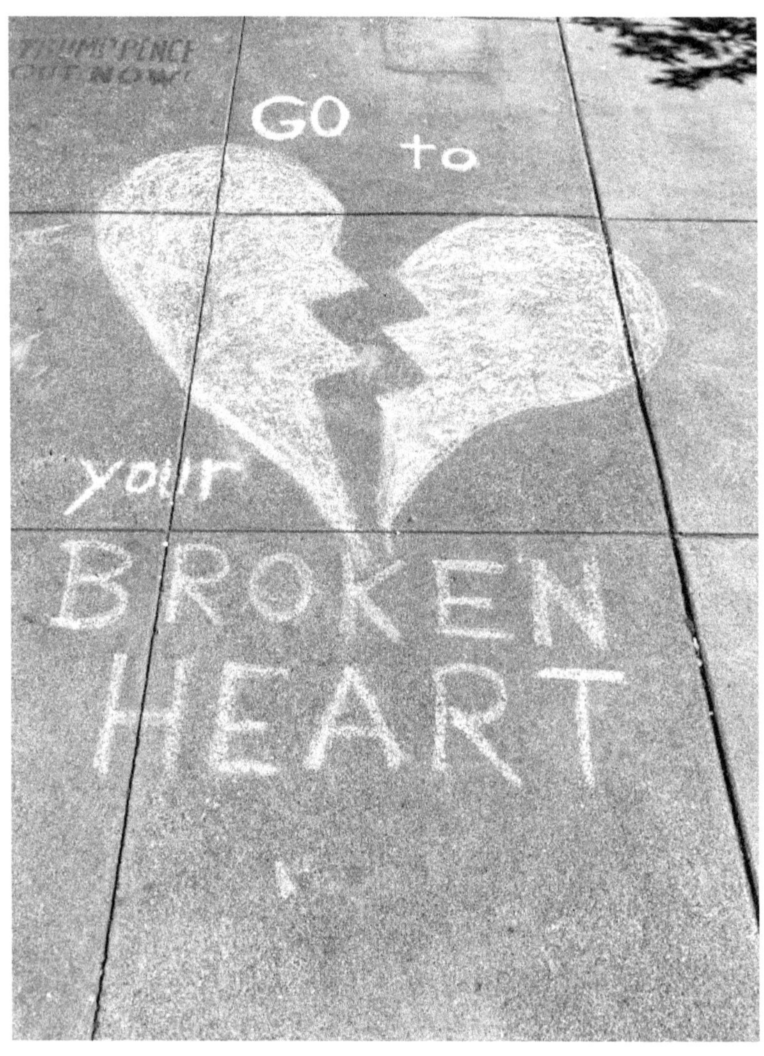

Agneta Falk, photo.
Kristina Brown, chalk.

LUIS GARCÍA *(El Salvador/USA)*

SOLACE

Her hands hold history,
in every crease, like rings on a tree.
A texture like brown bark, her skin is tough,
yet her touch is soft as a petal, caring.
Memories fall into the silent void.
Highlighted, black, expansive, deafening.
Metamorphosis looks different at each stage.
It serves its purpose.
There is a pining for the solace of nature.
It brings peace,
it also welcomes change.
You are meant to be free.

RAFAEL JESÚS GONZÁLEZ *(USA/Mexico)*

CUANDO LLORAN LOS ÁNGELES

A morte da floresta é o fim da *nossa vida*
a Dorothy Stang

En el arraigo de Bo Esperança
no lejos de Anapu, Pará, Brasil
mataron a la Hermana Dorothy.
Dora, ángel de la Amazona
a la vez que ella cogía su biblia
y decía las bendiciones.
Recuerda su nombre,
recuerda a Chico Mendes
y la multitud que murieron
en los 523 años de resistencia
defendiendo hogar y selva
sus nombres perdidos y demasiadas
las lenguas que los pronunciaban.
Los ganaderos, mineros, madereros
matan y no les importa la vida
ni, arrancándole los pulmones a la Tierra,
la Tierra misma; no oyen
cuando los ángeles lloran sabiendo
que la muerte de la selva
es el fin de nuestra vida; Se acorta el tiempo
y sigue la lucha. Recuerda
a Dorothy y todas las mártires por la Tierra
y hagamos nuestra revolución de amor feroz.

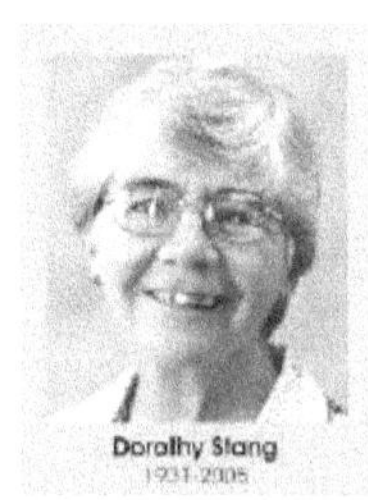

RAFAEL JESÚS GONZÁLEZ *(USA/Mexico)*

WHEN THE ANGELS WEEP

A morte da floresta é o fim da *nossa vida*
for Dorothy Stang

In the settlement of Bo Esperança
not far from Anapu, Pará, Brazil
they killed Sister Dorothy,
Dora, angel of the Amazon
as she held her bible
and said the beatitudes.
Remember her name,
remember Chico Mendes,
and the myriad who died
in 523 years of resistance
defending home & rainforest,
their names lost & far too many
the tongues that spoke them.
The ranchers, miners, loggers
kill & do not care for life
nor, tearing out the Earth's lungs,
for the Earth herself; they do not hear
when the angels weep knowing
that the death of the forest
is the end of our life. Time grows short,
& the struggle goes on. Remember
Dorothy & all the martyrs for the Earth
& let us make our revolution of fierce love.

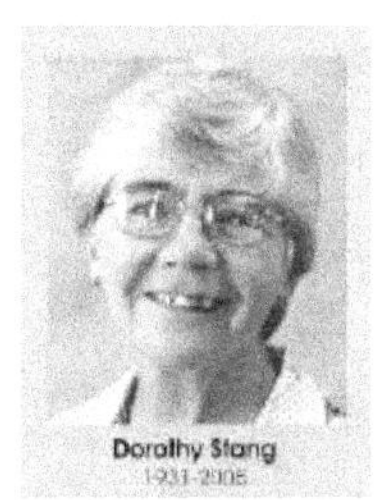

ART GOODTIMES

FOREMAN
ON THE FRONT LINES

He clung to the hood of the pickup
when the logger tried to run him down

Putting his wild life on the line
Standing in the path of the Machine

No small lawns of hope his vision
Nor bottom line profits *über alles*

But an interwoven braid of all creation
Putting Earth's flora fauna & funga first

Protests, demos, monkeywrenching work
His was a Neo-Luddite path to change

Unfurling cracks in a dam, campfire songs
Blocking roads to the tallest redwoods

Hoping to turn our Titantic hubris away
from the looming icebergs of collapse

To show the titans of industry what radical
really meant in defense of the Mother nest

Inspiring a generation to rewild this blue planet
using seeds of big ideas & brave symbolic deeds

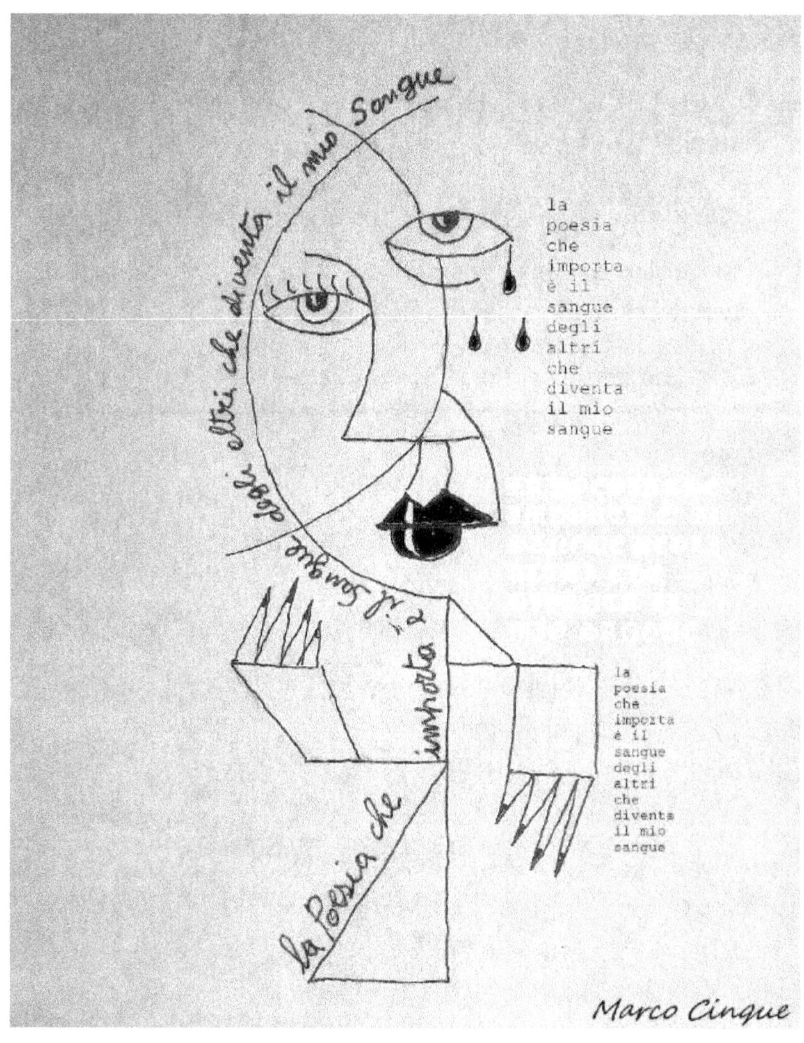

Marco Cinque

EGON GÜNTHER *(Germany)*

WEGZEICHEN

secret words & chants won't do any longer
lawrence ferlinghetti

nun gilt's

beiläufig

für andere pilger
worte fallen zu lassen

härter als stein
kälter als eis

damit sie dem beissenden wind
standhalten & dem wetter

die sonne darf sie nicht schmelzen
der frost nicht zerbrechen

sie mögen weiter nichts bezwecken
oder gar fruchten

auf kargem grund

sie sollen nur helfen
den weg zu markieren

im öden einerlei

das sich aus schutt
asche & knochen speist

EGON GÜNTHER *(Germany)*

WAYSIDE SIGN

secret words & chants won't do any longer
lawrence ferlinghetti

let's go

off the cuff

saying words casually
for other pilgrims

harder than stones
colder than ice

so that they stand up to the
biting wind & weather

the sun must not melt
nor the frost break them

they may not have any purpose
nor even be of use

on barren ground

they are to point
only the way

in the bleak daily grind

fed by rubble
ashes & bones

(Translated from German by Jörg W. Rademacher)

KAREN HARVEY-TURNER

KINDNESS EASES CHANGE

Octavia Butler said,
"Kindness eases change."

Kindness is not politeness,
Has nothing to do with the
Refinements of cities
Or the sophistications of society.

Kindness and compassion are twins,
Born of our connection to each other.
But kindness is the active one,
And acting in kindness,
Momentous or small,
It seeps into your pores,
And flows into the skin of strangers,
It is a medicine,
That alters you both
And helps remake the world.

BILL HATCH

IN THE MOMENT OF MOURNING

March with a limp
To the tunes of New Yorkers
Just how it is.

Ghost town my town
Never was no more
Then there or now.

Nostalgia will walk you
Back to my daydream
So baby, awake me.

I'm going to swing this town.
Sing down this town.
Swing down this town.

All I got left of the City
Is a Greek hat for poets
And a longshoreman's cap.

I play blues
In this white elders' chapel
When nobody else is around.

But like the old Greek said,
The greatest of harmonies
Doesn't make any sound.

We march in our souls
Our footsteps are soft
Our agony too silent

In the moment of mourning
When Time wanders
Like that roach on the wall

Who reminds you
You're living in dying
Dying in no time at all.

The gods are all dead
Hell's missiles target children
No messiah was ever called "Bibi."

The song chokes in the throat
And bounces off the wall
Between me and beautiful Mexico.

I can't wait to see
what our defenders of liberty
And worshippers of the Jesus

They strangle daily in his manger
(spellcheck cannot find "manger"
in its haystack)

Have cooked up for humanity
On a missile armed flotilla
Out on the South China Sea.

Recently, they say, a robot
Delivered a lengthy oration
On the virtues of AI.

We listened to its list
Of excellences: they did not include
Either hope, faith, or charity.

But that was the old theology
Like diplomacy was the old
Foreign relations.

Like democracy was the old
America. A dream as dead
As the dial telephone.

Like agriculture is the old economy.
Nothing must remain but
The high-tech, biotech, engine of growth.

But, in my soul,
There is a strong man
Moving furniture.

I live on hope
He will find
a plain arrangement

Because life's been tainted
By the time-stopping glamor
Of gaudy ideas.

Let Time begin again
Measured this time by grasses' growth
More rain, less fire, and love.

MARTIN HICKEL

THIS — THAT & THE OTHER

there is left & right & in-between
up — down & in the middle
good — bad & something neither
the best — the worst & second fiddle

also in & out & undecided
white & black & gray beside it
hot & cold & a room just right
light & dark & suddenly twilight

loud & silent & murmuring quiet
tall & short & simply average
hate & love & really no feeling
well & sick & hopefully healing

bright & dim & barely passing
sad or happy or sadly laughing
yes & no & maybe so
real or story — but who's to know

yet digital descriptions
only zero or one/go — no go
without intuition or feeling
brutally fixed choice/no choice

"ai" trained by minimal-wage
desperado contractors feeding
the insatiable machine dismal
assertions it endlessly craves

preset responses of private
overloaded oppressive property

actual "poop" — filling the world
up on capitalist propaganda

with absolutely no means of
any kind of an — "in between"
so — please tell me — darling
in a word — what's not to like...

JACK HIRSCHMAN

PATH

Go to your broken heart.
If you think you don't have one, get one.
To get one, be sincere.
Learn sincerity of intent by letting
life enter because you're helpless, really,
to do otherwise.
Even as you try escaping, let it take you
and tear you open
like a letter sent
like a sentence inside
you've waited for all your life
though you've committed nothing.
Let it send you up.
Let it break you, heart.
Broken-heartedness is the beginning
of all real reception.
The ear of humility hears beyond the gates.
See the gates opening.
Feel your hands going akimbo on your hips,
your mouth opening like a womb
giving birth to your voice for the first time.
Go singing whirling into the glory
of being ecstatically simple.
Write the poem.

EVERETT HOAGLAND

"EVERYTHING IS CONNECTED TO EVERYTHING ELSE"

— *Leonardo da Vinci*

All of us are, everything is, made of the cosmic dust
morphing all around us everywhere. Change being
the only constant in all existence. Be it

on the loose strands of our DNA on the hubbed, spoked
spinning wheel that is this world, solar system, galaxy,
universe. We need to see ourselves in all creation,

and all creation in ourselves, Ourselves in One Another.
Those of us who like connections made of similes
metaphors, symbols should know and show

all of us are, everything is already connected.
And that as the oceans go so go we.
As the air goes so go we.

As the forests go so go we.
As other life forms on Earth go so
go we. As our planet goes so go we. We

need to ACT on those understandings
so our ethics are our politics,
and our actions are

the afterlives of
our words.

SUSU JEFFREY

UNCLE SUGGIE

Uncle Suggie told me
he was going *Out West.*
Then he died. It was *an accident.*
I have a picture of Uncle Suggie
and me wearing his hat.
Uncle Suggie had bushy eyebrows
and when he laughed
he went sss—sss—sss—sss—sss
instead of ha—ha—ha.
Uncle Suggie was my first death.

I wanted to play the violin
but my parents said
If you want to play the violin
you'll take piano first for a year.

The piano looked like
Uncle Suggie's brown casket.
I couldn't even sit there
thinking about Uncle Suggie
who was cold when I touched his hand.

I hated to touch
the piano.
My parents said *if you really want*
to play the violin
you'll take piano for a year.

I really wanted to play the violin
so I borrowed a school one
for orchestra class
but the school called
my mother and said
did they want to rent

a school violin for me.
I got in trouble for sneaking
so I never learned
the violin.
I only got two
violin lessons.
They kept asking me
to come back to orchestra.

ZIBA KARBASSI *(Iran/UK)*

نووووف

نه
تو نمی توانی
به هیچ وجه من الوجود
ی
اگر راست می گویی
بگو ببینم

چند بار
برای شعر مرده ای

ZIBA KARBASSI *(Iran/UK)*

NOOOOOF

No
You cannot
Under no condition
In no way possible
Not in any dimension of existence
Divert or distract me
From my path
If you are so sure of yourself
If you're telling the truth
Tell me
Til' now
How many times have you died
For a poem

(Translated from Farsi by Nazlee Radboy and Ziba Karbassi)

ELIOT KATZ

IMAGINE AGAIN

Imagine
a de-militarized
Middle
East
and
then
imagine
a completely
de-militarized
world.
It's not
so
easy
these
days,
but
please
try.

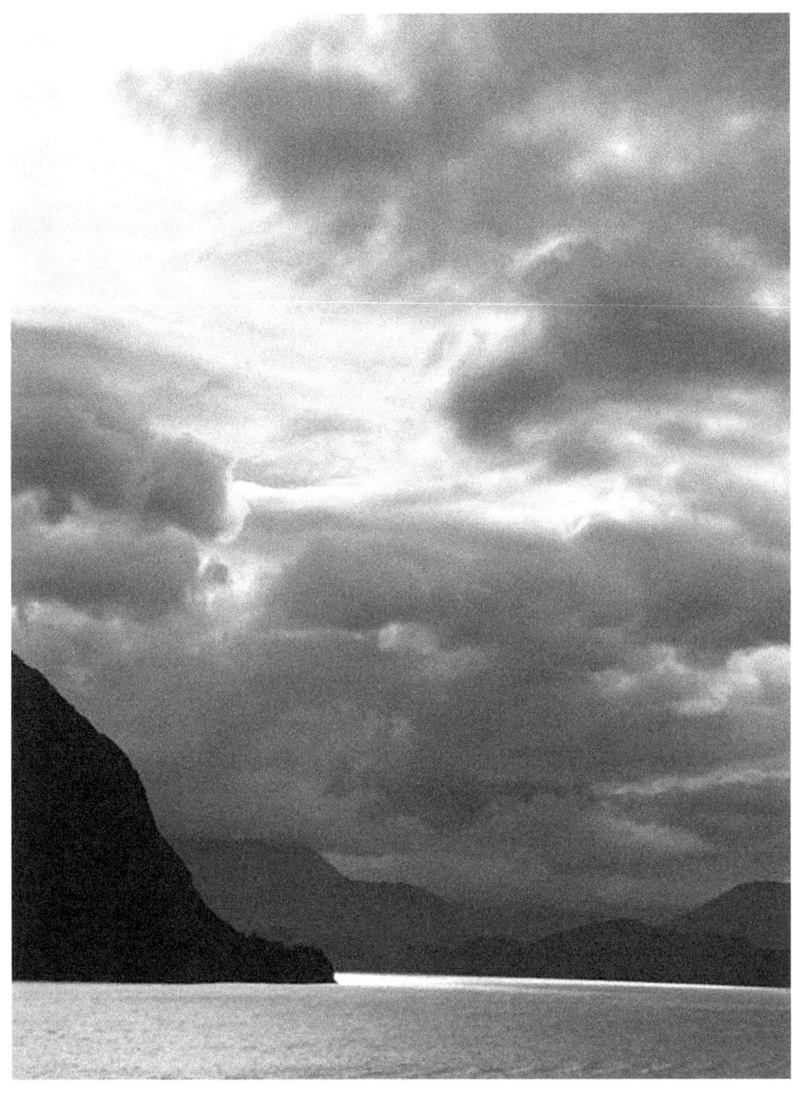

Cathleen Williams

KUSAL KURUVITAGE *(Sri Lanka)*

නගර සැලසුම

සුසානය අලංකෘත කර උද්‍යානයක් මෙන
මැතිරූ ඉදි කර අඳුරු මූසල ගතිය දුරු කර
මාසෙ පඩියේ අවසාන් කටයුතු කර
මැළවුණු මුහුණින් බිම බලාගෙන ගෙදර එන
නුවරැති නිසල අරණක් ය අද සුසානය
ආණ්ඩුව ඔබ වෙනුවෙන් ම නිම කළ

KUSAL KURUVITAGE *(Sri Lanka)*

CITY PLAN

The grave yard has been beautified
Like a park
The dark gloomy look has been
Dispelled and pathways made
The grave yard has turned into
A silent forest within the city
One made specially for you by the government
You, who have laid to rest
Your entire monthly wages
And are now walking home with downcast eyes
And your
Furrowed face

(Translated from Sinhala by Vivimarie VanderPoorten)

D.L. LANG

DISOBEDIENCE IS LOVE

When the law enforces injustice,
upholding and fueling corruption,
then being an outlaw is righteous,
and rebellion is our only path to freedom.

Follow your heart and not immoral orders!
When they demand you fall in line, disobey!
Light bonfires of inner strength and courage!

When they fan the flames of fear, disobey!
Walk forward fueled by love and solidarity.
When they teach you who to hate, disobey!

Disobedience is love when fascists call the shots.
As they tighten their grip upon our neighbors,
we must fight back against this cancer of hatred.
Only love of humanity can light the way forward.

JENNIFER LEONG

MASKETEERS

is there only disharmony
from variants of cacophony
are they masquerading as musketeers
in actuality, manipulating spears
spearheading scammers and phonies
who murder myriad melodies
who pretend to make connections
within and inter-generations

they fence off areas and create walls
agents for gravity in its quest for falls
is there more behind all of these
where they boast and feast as beasts
on others' misfortunes and mishaps
was there a time, primordial perhaps
which formed or misinformed
such behavior to make it their norm

at what level, when did this happen
at what point did this portal open
for bullies to reign in icy businesses
powers rulers predators protractors
no one is another's protector
doubtless, everyone hates losers
each person cares and defends
his own only while others he offends

is there anyone who could be a quilter
among so many would-be quitters
one who weaves the tapestry together
instead of tearing apart members

of the same body of humanity
who believes in lifting the community
who fends not for oneself only
who cares for parity for another party

who activates a one-for-all creativity
not an all-for-one rush mentality
crushing others with the same goal
to reach the podium for gold
is someone out there somewhere
an angel who bothers to spare
a thought offers to alleviate
brothers' burdens before it's too late

LI-MING LEONG *(Singapore)*

WORKPLACE WARFARE

This is a Cold War,
It is them or us,
And we are losing.

Each day in this office,
This hellhole with fluorescent lighting,
We become less and less ourselves,
Chipped away in infinitesimal specks,
Dying the death of a thousand paper cuts.

Look! There goes one!
A trivialising comment on a painstakingly put-together
proposal,
Another! The twenty-second (or is it twenty-sixth?)
iteration of a PowerPoint deck marked with a
casual "Revise"...
All those reports lying fallow in my manager's desk drawer,
Never a glance, nor once chanced upon.

You need to find your tribe, kakak[1],
Is it Don from IT behind the designer dendrobium?
Or Hwee Ling, sales superstar?
Shall we have lunch?

Who to sakar[2], angkat bola[3]?
Like everyone but everyone,
Knows about Alice in Senior Management,
She can tekan[4]you with the best,
But she loves a good solid budget put together just so,
Oh, Oh, Oooh,
Just act like you like it,

Even if you are not feeling it,
Maybe, especially so, bro...

Only here, in frozen florescent fairyland,
Do we troglydytes crouch daily in cubicles,
Creating an atmosphere so frosty,
The airconditioned air coalesces into icy glances drawn
like flying daggers,
As Masters of Taichi[5] fling their burdens like arrows,
The magic of their martial arts
Guaranteeing them the celestial rewards of worklife-
balance,
As the rest of us look on in awe,
Recognising our lack,
As we lie bleeding,
Time's sand dribbling from
The many knives in our back.

Yet even when coiled sobbing
In the dubious foxhole of a latrine,
Suffering PTSD from work and meeting burnout,
We tell ourselves not to be Disney Princesses,
After all, we can fend off
The Monday Morning monsters
With designer caramel lattes
Dribbled twice with pumpkin spice.

"How can this compare with real warzones,
Real wounds, abuse and death?", we laugh.
The hum of a hundred monitors replies,
"It is self-doubt, spooling like piled printouts,
It is learned helplessness from too many crushed ideals,
It is the panic of constant unreasonable expectations,
And the unblinking abuse of power,
Transmitted down an unthinking hierarchy.

Above all, it is the dis-ease of human condition,
The disease of human condition,
That justifies any and all actions,
Because 'they' are wrong,
And 'they' have wronged us,
Or 'they' will,
Or 'they' can,
Can't they?"

After all, this is a Cold War,
It is them or us,
And we are losing.

<u>Translation for Singlish words</u>

Kakak – (Malay) Sister
Sakar – (Malay) Lit. means sweet. Colloquial use means to butter up someone.
Angkat Bolah – (Malay) Lit. means carry balls. Colloquail use means to curry favour in a servile way.
Tekan – (Malay) Lit. means to press. Colloquail use means to torture or bully.
Taichi – (Chin) Its a martial art. Colloquail use means to push a task or responsibility to someone else.
Offices in Singapore usually have the air-conditioning set to freezing temperatures, hence the reference to a "Cold War" but of course there are plenty of other meanings as well!

MARK LIPMAN

FOR ALL THE MOTHERS' TEARS

For all those unseen
hiding beneath the rubble
whose children are double amputees,
just statistics for the war machine

For all those who can't speak,
who've been silenced and shut out
from the national debate

For all those made homeless
by the bombs of indifference,
targeted by sniper and settlement,
the red ink in the ledgers
of a blood-for-profit regime

For all the hostages
lingering in black sites and prison cells
held without charge or trial
hidden away from the spotlight

For all those being starved
and left hungry, those guilty
of being born, of being a thorn
in the side of Democracy

For all those who've ever
picked up a rock
or spray-painted graffiti
who've lifted up their voices
and their middle fingers
to the capitalist patriarchy

For all those who've decolonized
their brains and stood
on the right side of history

This poem is for you.

OSCAR LOCATELLI *(Italy)*

META' FORA E META' DENTRO

Ho avuto fame
e mi avete dato
un buono-sconto.

Ho avuto sete
e mi avete consigliato
un happy-hour.

Ero forestiero
e mi avete indicato
un resort,

nudo
e mi avete segnalato
una influencer,

malato
e mi avete detto
una preghiera.

OSCAR LOCATELLI *(Italy)*

HALF OUTSIDE AND HALF INSIDE, METAPHOR.

I was hungry
and you gave me
a coupon.

I was thirsty
and you advised me
a happy hour.

I was a stranger
and you pointed me
a resort,

naked
and you reported me
an influencer,

sick
and you told me
a prayer.

ANNA LOMBARDO *(Italy)*

COME POSSIAMO RIPROMETTERCI UMANI?

Una geniale cecità in groppa a droni
mescola Reality, torti e ragioni
statistiche di cadaveri, merletti e rossetti,
bandiere e croci. Nei cimiteri
orrori ed errori, benedetti e assolti.
Sangue lascivo scivola intanto
su crolli, detriti, volti, gambe, mani
con fabbriche di armi da cornice
a bocche spalancate di case, accampamenti,
fragili ossa di bimbi e bimbe e un alfabeto
che fa fatica a domandare: ma come possiamo
riprometterci umani?

ANNA LOMBARDO *(Italy)*

HOW WE CAN PROMISE OURSELVES THAT WE ARE STILL HUMAN?

A brilliant blindness on the back of drones
mixes Reality, wrongs and rights,
statistics of corpses, lace and lipsticks,
flags and crosses. In all cemeteries
horrors and errors are blessed and absolved.
Meanwhile blood slides lasciviously
on blasts, debris, faces, legs, hands,
and weapons factories as a backdrop
at wide open mouths of houses, camps,
fragile bones of boys and girls, and an alphabet
which hardly asks how we can promise
ourselves that we are still human?

KIRK LUMPKIN

Ask Why? (a rap)

You don't grow up,
you just give up
when you quit
asking why
Don't you know that you better
Keep alive/keep alive/keep alive
Don't you know that you better/keep alive
Keep alive/the question why
Ask why, ask why, ask why, Because
it helps to inform us both
you and I
Ask why, ask why, ask why, Because
every time you don't there's a
little bit you die
Ask why, ask why, ask why, Because
there'll always be more
to which it will apply
Ask why, ask why, ask why, Because
it can help you focus
with your own eye
Ask why, ask why, ask why, Because
it could help you understand the place
you occupy
Ask why, ask why, ask why, Because
There is so much junk they want
us to buy
Ask why, ask why, ask why, Because
it can help you deal with what
makes you cry
Ask why, ask why, ask why, Because
police have made another

unarmed black man die
Ask why, ask why, ask why, Because
it helps to tell the difference
between truth and lie
Ask why, ask why, ask why, Because
there's a lot you won't learn
if this you do not try
Ask why, ask why, ask why, Because
those that think they run world
want you to be shy
Ask why, ask why, ask why, Because
you cannot trust a government
that on you spies
Ask why, ask why, ask why, Because
without incisive questions
things rigidify
Ask why, ask why, ask why, Because
it's the kind of word
that you can make your ally
Ask why, ask why, ask why, Because
they'll want to go to war and many
innocents will die
Ask why, ask why, ask why, Because
answers light you up
like you're a fire fly
Ask why, ask why, ask why, Because
wonder isn't childish
it's the original high
Ask why, ask why, ask why, ask why, ask why
You don't grow up,
you just give up
when you quit
asking why

BIPLAB MAJEE *(India)*

আমাদের কারো হাতে নেই অনন্ত সময়

বিপ্লব মাজী

> ["আমাদের জীবনের মধ্য দিয়ে যাওয়া প্রতিটি মানুষই অনন্য। তারা সবসময় নিজেদের কিছু রেখে যায় এবং তাদের সাথে আমাদের কিছুটা নিয়ে যায়। সেখানে তারা থাকবে যারা অনেক কিছু নেবে, কিন্তু তারা থাকবে না যারা আমাদের কিছুই ছেড়ে যাবে না। এটা স্পষ্ট প্রমাণ যে "দুটি আত্মা আকস্মিকভাবে মিলিত হয় না।"
>
> —হোর্হে লুইস বোর্হেস।]

আমাদের কারো হাতে নেই
অনন্ত সময়,
জন্মের মুহূর্ত থেকে
বালিঘড়িতে
মেপে দেওয়া হয়েছে জীবন

এ গ্রহটিতে তুমি
কতদিন থাকবে?
মায়ায় বেঁধোনা কাউকে
কেউ কারো না,
শুধু এক অনির্দিষ্ট পথে গন্তব্য সবার।

যদিও ভালোবাসার নির্যাস
একমাত্র এ পৃথিবীতেই পাওয়া যায়।

অতএব, যতদিন পারা যায় বাঁচো,
বাঁচার আনন্দে বাঁচো,
ভুলে যাও মৃত্যুর কথা,
যখন মৃত্যু আসবে
কাউকে না জানিয়েই আসবে।

পৃথিবীতে থেকে যাবে
স্মৃতির প্রতিটি পৃষ্ঠা।

BIPLAB MAJEE *(India)*

NO ONE HAS ENDLESS TIME WITH THEM

> *"Every person who passes through our lives is unique. They always leave something of themselves and take a little of us with them. There will be those who take a lot, but there will not be those who leave us nothing. It is clear evidence that "two Souls do not meet by chance."*
>
> *—Jorge Luis Borges*

We don't have endless time with us
Life has been measured
By a sand-glass from the very moment of birth

How long would you be here on this planet?
So don't be attached with anyone
None of us belong to anybody
Everyone is destined to an uncertain path.

Though the essence of love
is available only in this earth.

So live as much as possible
Live to enjoy the happiness
Forget about death
Death comes
Without intimating to any one.

Each page of memory
Remains on this earth.

(Translated from Bengali by Nandita Bhattacharya.)

ELIZABETH MARINO

A WOMAN DRAPED IN POWER

> *"I believe protest is important.... I wish I could be in Gaza and stand in front of a Palestinian family and be strong enough to protect them."*
>
> South African Foreign Minister Naledi Pandoa
> on Zeteo.com (21 March 2024)

This woman draped in power
Is speaking. History rests in her lap.

Lifting her head to directly
Meet her interlocutor's queries

With deft policy parries, a firm gaze
Lilting formal diction. A smile.

She had entered the room
Filled with artificial light

Knowing full well the depths
Of darkness just outside.

Still, her hands push against the walls
Sure the structures will hold.

ÁNGEL L. MARTÍNEZ

ORCHESTRA IN A CITY CANYON

After the Chaos,
crowded downtowns turned into quiet wastelands
What remained of crumbling buildings,
bricks and mortar heavily damaged
by collapsed pieces of glass and steel,
remained stark reminders
of where masses once walked
and where the old rich thought
they would rule forever

Now, forever belongs to these city canyons
There remain those who have chosen to work these streets,
not in toil but with joy
Once again they could hear
the waves of the bay,
the lapping of the river,
Alongside the calls of cats
whose families inhabit holes in the walls
and the silence of dogs unleashed, running free,
in packs in large empty spaces
Abandoned cars, rusted,
with cloud-dusted windows, cats hide there too

Chaos won. Money lost.
The true winners of these spaces
were scores of musicians, wanderers of the streets
Some played on corners
Some occupied parks,
sitting on benches of peeled wood and plastic,
serenading all animals around

Musicians who found their way
to where once money was god
now guided by the spirit
of tones arising from pavements
One day, harmony happened
One horn, then two, filled the air
up to the cracks in the buildings
A swell of baritone and bass saxes
emerged from these improvised stages
The deep drones broken by occasional spurts
of high notes
rising in the air, first shot straight up,
then flourishes of notes ascending and descending
in forms like invisible question marks,
even upside-down

Drums soon entered across distances
as drummers have always done across time
Basses emerged in waves of rumbles and slides
Guitars as evocations of the space above
All percussion as evocations of the space below
Keys of all sizes, some linked
to the few live electrical outlets still there

No conductor. No composer.
Every song was new
Every player wrote the songs
And carried on the tradition

CINDY MATTHEWS

DUST FROM GAZA

The air quality index is higher than it's ever been
The particulate count is sky high
No fires burning in California or out west currently
Could this be dust from Gaza?

I breathe in the air full of particulates and cough and groan
Where has all the oxygen gone?
Has it been burned up in thousands of fires caused by
Israeli bombing?
Could this be caused by dust from Gaza?

It is said that matter is neither created nor destroyed
That we are breathing in air that was once breathed out by
pharaohs and kings
That every speck of soot clinging to our car windows isn't
original
Could these gray motes be dust from Gaza?

Every morning I check the air quality index
Every day since October the number has been in the
moderate to unhealthy range
Once a day I take my asthma medication and think—
Am I breathing in dust from Gaza?

What air do Gazans breathe in?
What air do Zionists breathe in?
Are we all not breathing in the same air?
Why are Americans allowing the IDF to disintegrate an
entire people, turning them to dust?
For our penance this Ash Wednesday we should be
covered in dust from Gaza

TOMMI AVICOLLI MECCA

WHEN SOLDIERS LAY DOWN

when soldiers lay
down all their arms and
say no
and the guns and the
bombs disappear
like the snow
and the pentagon's
a crumbling old ruin
you know
and the generals are
using a tractor and hoe

when the rows of white
crosses are no longer
seen
and the enlisted come
back to lives so routine
and the children stop
playing with guns
and war toys
and the movies don't
teach us that war is
a joy

when the skies are
not screaming with
angels of blue
and revenge is not
sweet like a fat
honeydew
when peace is admired
and war is obscene
and all that I'm writing
is not just a dream

KAREN MELANDER-MAGOON

HOME

The world is full of homeless
Some scrambling in cities
That once housed them
Some waking up to empty skies
Where tents had been removed
While they slept
Some waking to rubble
Where homes once had been
Where the dead accompanied their slumber
The world is full of homeless
And full of bounty
To house and feed those in want
To bring peace to families
Frightened or destroyed by war
To wrap the wounds
To cure the ill
To feed the hungry
To hug and warm the babies
Who have barely seen the world
Beyond the womb they left
Bereft of all they might expect
Of love and hope
The world is full of homeless
Full of sorrow
Full of grief
Bestowed upon the innocent
The world cries out in anguish
This is not my world
I am joy
I am beauty
I am love

I am a home for all
Restore me
So all may find hope
Restore me
So all may find peace
Restore me
So all may find love
Restore me
So all may find home
In my arms.

SARAH MENEFEE

BLINK

businesses
large and small
come and go

(with every blink)

but there he still goes by
on the rags of his toes

(it's amazing!)
as seasons come and go

TUREEDA MIKELL

III PART RECIPE TO VIRTUAL REALITY

I

Gather one group of astrophysicists and physicists
Separate 3 parts physicist to 2 parts astrophysicist
Split right and left brain hemispheres
Pair *Never let the right hand know what the left is doing*
Ooze into a time capsule
Allow decades to prepare

II

Stir in 100% academic self-entitlement
100% non-systemic English conditioners with
100% queen Liz defender of a faith
Wrap in One god, One fate, One baptism
Detach Sky chief from women children family
Break female from holy trinity
Debone natural conceptions ability
Collect Adam Eve Mary Joseph stories
Steep them in artificial insemination
Salt flesh heavily in Sin,
Mark missed, born broken,
Cure virgins, women, and nuns in husband Jesus
Strip sexuality ...Bathe in virtual reality
Look but don't feel, smell but don't taste
Whip in self-flagellation, sensory deprivation
Add, *you can't have your cake and eat it too*
Prepare one reel each of
Frankenstein Step-ford Wives stew
View until contradictions thicken
Combine hegemony's lex-is-con,
Hex will run non-causal micro aggressions.

III

Shred hormone receptors, use
5G magnetic synthetics, chemicals, plastics
Extract nouns from verbs
Inculcate war is peace,
Slavery is freedom,
Ignorance is strength, mix well
Coat in public relations house of persuasion
Repeat 7times for adults 14 times for children
Bind throat & feet before broiling
Watch what's said and done before boiling

Allow neck to stiffen in attrition
Simmer until bipolarism ascends
Skim magnetic poles ...dislocate soul
Crystalize dissonance in canine-dog obedience
 Fetch, heel, stay, obey
Poach the field they're in or play
Manifest destiny will activate new reality and
Change public values accordingly
With consumers oblivious, autistic, lustfully numb
   Renunciating survival instinct they will become
     Corporate futures, monetized for their blindness!

This sugar high ice tea was brought to you by
 The Law of exclusion
   Masters of Biz Science
    Where sterilizing the public's mind
     Without their knowledge
       Is their most important product.

NANCY MOREJÓN *(Cuba)*

NIÑA SALIENDO DE GUINEA

"Cambiábamos de país, como de zapatos"
Bertold Brecht

Tengo ocho años.
Nací en Guinea, como mis padres.
Me quedé dormida esperando el avión
y nunca más los volví a ver.
Íbamos rumbo a Nueva York
sin pasar por Tierra-Firme,
sin cruzar el Tapón del Darién,
sin caminar sobre las aguas del Río Bravo.

Me quedé dormida y, cuando desperté, ya mis padres no estaban.

Vi luces de neón y recorrí todas las salidas del aeropuerto.

Tuve hambre por la mañana en la puerta 7.
Tuve hambre por la tarde en la puerta D36.
Tuve hambre por la noche en la puerta C22.

Tenía hambre y sed.

Al lado, vendían quesos bien envueltos con jamón del diablo.
Comí dos.

Al otro lado, había una tienda donde vendían
tennis y *jacquets* perfumados.

Sin darme cuenta, reposé en los asientos muchas horas.
Dormí como un lirón.

NANCY MOREJÓN *(Cuba)*

LITTLE GIRL LEAVING GUINEA

"We change countries like we change shoes."
Bertold Brecht

I'm eight years old.
I was born in Guinea, like my parents.
I fell asleep waiting for an airplane
and I never saw them again.
We were going to New York
without passing through Tierra-Firme
without crossing the Darien Gap,
without walking through the waters of the Rio Grande.

I was still sleeping and, when I woke up, my parents were not there.

I saw neon lights and ran from one to another of all the airport exits.

I was hungry in the morning at Gate 7.
I was hungry in the afternoon at Gate D36
I was hungry at night at Gate C22.

I was hungry and thirsty.

On one side they were selling cheese well wrapped with ham
I ate two.

On the other side, there was a store that sold
tennis shoes and perfumed jackets.

Without realizing it, I curled up in the seat for many hours.
I slept like a dormouse.

Me quedé dormida... sin saberlo.
Me despertó un señor vestido de uniforme:
"—¿Dónde están mi papá y mi mamá?
Pensé que usted vendría a darme noticias suyas".
"—¿Dónde están papá y mamá?", le volví a preguntar, casi rendida.

Tengo ocho años y nací en Guinea.

I stayed asleep – without knowing it.
A man in a uniform woke me up:
"Where are my mother and father?
I thought you were coming to give me news about them."
"Where are daddy and mommy? I asked him again,
almost giving up.

I'm eight years old and was born in Guinea.

(Translated from Spanish by Barbara Paschke)

EDWARD MYCUE

THE OLD PHOENIX MEETS THE NEW TRIO

1. THE FINAL FINAL FINAL TIME MY ROOT, ROUTES, RANGES
was sung from over-influences going back through those years before those under-influenced go off track to blank slates* before going forward on through surrender from birth starting bald to hairy high jinks growing-years that start all the crazy crazed futured musical functionings before clouds thickened clearly a mind walking alive in monster bellies in our by my lifetimes is still ahead of me today at the edge near falling since my comprehension's tiny. So stop my madness tonight as my mind grows like a jack in the beanstalk bean as here's a flattened floating balloon.

*Oliver Wendell Holmes, Sr: The Poet at the Breakfast Table (1872) wrote, "We are all tattooed in our cradles with the beliefs of our tribe; the record may seem superficial, but it is indelible."

*"We start transparent, and then the cloud thickens. All history back our pane of glass...." (Virginia Woolf's novel, Jacob's Room, Hogarth Press 1922, London)

2. BECOMING SO TIRED OF LEGACIES

Making sense of the awareness of our connections and distances is chance and is choice. The culture you find yourself within may not be welcoming to whatever your kind may seem to be that you will learn you are a part of and may or maybe not choose to accept.

Were you freed from community restrictions that may not always like as you are and do, no-no's to others, you might have never started examining the ways you are different.

Looking into and exploring the kind of world and the specific culture you exist in is not a "clean slate" for you. The past shapes you and everybody else. But it steals your life.

At the end of the day what's good for you may be a separating into newness that can enact too great a loss from who and what you're accustomed loving, loved by others.

To live and love without conditions may be like with or without coffee you learned to like. Few persons end up living in a Nordic Summer that they didn't make. But the most are fine.

Okay, but an oddball like your self who doesn't fit in, should you try, will live. Your inauthentic life will in some time become so tired of legacies following the crowd.

3. COME BACK PEOPLE, FRIENDS, LISTEN

What could never end might yet still come again
Years turn, hope spins again into morning
Fleeing, finding stars, sky, sirens screaming
One frail and fragrant puff of finished fuse

Scooping from that mist of muffled bones

The tired half-dreams of a failed dream,

Fragmenting, shattering, grinding-down
Time the phoenix entered the sun dance

Smoke clouding what passes, these keys of flesh,

Razing memories of the flower years,

Scorching fog, fuchsia, western laurel tree
Crackling embers into singeing song
All that noisy night the phoenix flames

MAJID NACIFY *(Iran/USA)*

GAZA REVEILLE

There, they sell dreams:
One for returning to the "Promised Land"
And the other to revive the "Caliphate."
What is forgotten
Is humanity.
Children put in danger by one side
Are being blown up by the other.

Abandon your bloody nightmares
Let the future
Free itself
From the yoke of the past
And two nations
Live side by side.
Wake up!
Wake up!

BILL NEVINS

International Poetry Day—NOT A GOOD DAY IN GAZA

"They took all our land."—John Trudell

The hell you say "peace" today,
when the Palestine people starve

and walk to the wire
and it is NOT
a "good day to die"!

So you weep for the poor
poor
Indios of America
oh you weep
they were so poor
they were so brave

they are so dead
and
Custer was a bad man
so bad
and
those days of Wounded Knee in 1890 and 1973
were both so sad

you weep
you compose poems
laced with your tears
for Anna Mae,
for all those people
those poor Indio people

yet . . . today . . .yet . . .
yet
when the people rise
when the people walk

to the wire
when the people
do not stop
when the people
when the people bleed
starve
die
in their dozens
in their hundreds
in their thousands
you sit
on your pampered poetic
arse
and you dream
of peace
and you send out little
Facebook hearts . . .
and you blame Hamas
and you blame Iran
and you blame "white liberals"
when the people are gunned down and bombed
and starved
and you dare to say that those who criticize Likud and
Netanyahu
are abusing their "white privilege"
you say hey
it is extremists
who caused that
killing
and extremists
must die
should die

will die
you say hey
I don't like extremists
who walk up to sniper bullets
and die
you say hey
I love the Indios
they are not extremists
they are so nice
they know when it is
a good day

to
die
you write of flowers
and
peace
and
your momma
and
you say Hamas did it Iran did it
Israel didn't do it
it is antisemitic to say Israel did it

you say both sides are not nice
but one side is nicer than another

you, oh
sweet poetic you—
you are so nice
aren't you?
and John Trudell weeps
for the dead and dying at the Gaza wall,
in his grave
in his grave.

JEFF NOWAK

A RESPONSE FROM THE SUPREME COURT

Protests ring round every door.
Prophets all see signs
of fiery death and doom and muddled lore,
but everything is fine.

I know this.
You chose me.
This means you have to trust me.
In a crowded room, you'd see me,
and hastily approach me
and tell me
everything that's wrong
with immigrants and voters' rights
and all the crime and crazies
with a thousand other grievances
and babies.
You can't forget the babies.

Calm down.
I'm on it.
I feel what you see.
I'll fix your every fault with force
while you can merely be.

The refugees have all been searched.
The papers have been signed.
The bombs are waiting in the sky.
Everything is fine.

SERENA PICCOLI

THE STATE OF CONTROL

to Julian Assange

They made me live in an adorable illusion
where I used to have butter and nettle at breakfast

they were living next to me
sipping the soup suspiciously
always with rule and divide in their mind

They injected me with the venom of ecstasy I believed
everything they said
all was perfect

they kept an ear and eye
all the time
for my own sake, they say

the State of control

don't move\don't speak
move and speak like they say

Unlike Assange
who enlightened us
They keep him alive and dead like the Schrödinger's cat

And while they bribe and hide
they fear us
tremble
spit the fat broth
we are in their way
to see the end of the ghosts of the fleas

GREGORY POND

PRAY FOR

i pray for peace
        for war to cease
        for kids to breathe
        for love's increase

i pray for youth
        for guns to truce
        for hate to lose
        for freedom, too

i pray for calm
        for respite from harm
        for bombs to disarm
        for cold hearts to warm

i pray for strife's end
        for foe to turn friend
        for this message to send
        for a better world,
                                        amen

KATHY POWERS

NO SERVICE HERE

Where will we go
To get our food stamps?
Where will we go?
Follow the rules.

Where can we go to?
Where is the person
Who tells us if we live or die?

When did this happen?
We got no notice.
Why did this happen?
We need some answers.

Is there an answer
In our new chaos
That tells us if we'll live or die?

Where do we go?
How will we get there?
We have no bus fare?
How can we go?

Pushed to the edge of
Chicago's west side
Six miles across the city

Where does the truth lie?
How can we live?
How will we die?
Tell us why!

Tell us where!
Tell us how!
Tell us why!
Tell us why!

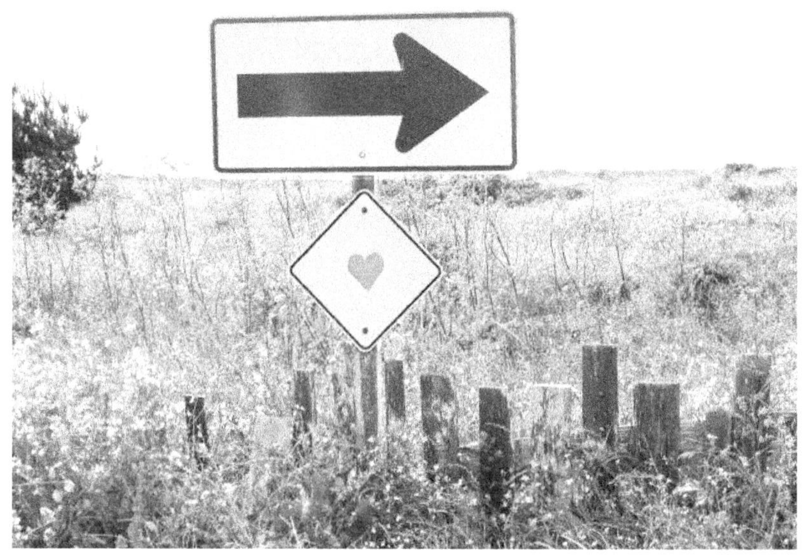

Andrena Zawinski

THORWALD PROLL

ROUNDING UP, PLEASE

"The Sleep of Reason
gives Birth to Monsters"
you don't have to
learn this anymore
I'm crumpling the
Newspaper because they
don't bring what's
in the Stars
on the Ferry
to Nowhere
there is an
Atmosphere of
soulless
Modern Times
the Senator she's
stuck in Traffic Jams
hard-hearted
Policemen
club the Road
clear for her
I'm in Front of
the Restaurant like
in Front of the Entrance
to Paradise
if I now enter I'm
lost forever
the Ball bounces
out of Bounds
to the Loser
the Hair stands on
and
the Rain
sets in
the decreasing

Moon looks like
van Gogh's
cut off Ear
it's early
in the Morning and
one lives when
the World is dying
and spoiling

MARGARET RANDALL

THE FAIRYTALE

In that high mountain world
left after flood and fire
destroyed earth's lowlands,
a mother reads a bedtime story
to her child.

The screaming digital games
of her own youth
were silenced long ago.
A few cherished books survive,
deep comfort now.

The mother reads about an army
of wicked men called presidents.
They lied and cheated until
all power was theirs,
life itself at risk.

They targeted women especially—
the mother shudders
as she reads. But those presidents
didn't count on the power
of our resistance.

The mother smiles as she tucks
a frayed blanket about
her child's sleepy body.
The child squirms in anticipation
of the story's end.

She knows it by heart: All women
unite to achieve survival
even as they mourn their dead.
The story brings joy
but also dread

to the child about to fall asleep,
so the mother,
fearing her child's fear,
reminds her it's just a fairytale
after all.

D. A. "ROARSHOCK" WILSON

HONG KONG TRANSFER

The Union Jack comes down
the Chinese flag goes up
probably no opium in the hall.
Prince Charles makes jolly
with Jiang Zemin.
If the soldiers march
with such precision...
Live via C-Span on
Chinese National Television
- English Service - from Beijing -
Cut to music
young woman dancing
softly fluttering as new butterflies
in Tiananmen Square
all lovely smiles
pretty feet lightly tripping
over the ghost of blood
and the slumbering spirit
of the Goddess of Democracy.

(San Francisco, June 30, 1997 -
July 1, in Hong Kong and Beijing)

LEW ROSENBAUM

GHOSTS OF THOMAS PAINE

> *"Of more worth is one honest man to society ...*
> *than all the crowned ruffians who ever lived."*
> —Thomas Paine

Of more worth
is one honest Tortuguita
to society
than all the Cop City builders
in America

Of more worth to society
is one honest poet
than all the lap-dog journalists
celebrating the crowned
Capitol ruffians

Of more worth
is one honest communist
to society
than all the vampiring Bezoses,
the Goldman Sachses,
crowned by lechery, greed,
and outright murder

Let the ghosts of Tom Paine
stalk the streets of America
preaching common sense
to overturn the divine right
of private property

NICK SAMARAS

LOWANI UNDER TWO MOONS

Your food is not my culture,
but I come to love your food as well as my own.

England used to be the whitest country
with its bangers and mash, its pale staples of starch and protein.

Yet even England has now embraced its national
favourite cuisine of curry and flavouring for the palate.

How we went from our old moon in our torn hemisphere
to this new moon over a new hemisphere. How the colonies

slowly conquer the Empires, relaxing the taste-buds,
opening the collective mind to experience. Perhaps, then,

there is no such thing as race. No such thing as race but culture,
a blending of foods and fragrant spices: tamarind, turmeric,

saffron and cumin. Look. Even in war, even in exile,
here is what we managed to bring from the shrapnel of our lives

and the body of our homelands: recipes, bright clothing,
dance-steps, a joy of hospitality, a way of mixing to live in
safety.

Help us set a new table, and may it enlarge and bless
your own tables and homes in this sheltered land.

SANDRO SARDELLA *(Italy)*

affioramenti 3

"il silenzio è talmente preciso"
—Mark Rothko

solo rumore di pioggia.   tace quel canto
una lampadina   accendi la radio
svuota il portacenere di muscoli esibiti
nell'industria della guerra dei profitti
rompere   i passi   il silenzio
in fondo al cuore era babele era babilonia
era cielo caduto   puoi chiederlo al vento
era deserto era tramonto
era vuota stella d'occidente sulla città che brucia
qualcosa   qualcuno.   bagliori appena
col viso rivolto alle stelle
l'acqua scorre.   luce lenta
cosa vuoi che faccia con le mie parole?
cosa devo scrivere?
in paesaggi grigi con acque avvelenate
macerie di scheletri di cementi
mi fanno male gli occhi.   storie operaie
crollo di cantiere a Firenze.   poi le grida
ogni numero nasconde nomi e storie
la vergognosa classifica dei morti
bolle di sapone
nel clamore di.   un cagare soldi
non può   non deve tacere la poesia
inseguire il sole
un brivido la preghiera
senti le rane che cantano
dove si balla   per riscaldarsi dal freddo
scrivimi   quando arrivi a casa
mi nutro della tua assenza

SANDRO SARDELLA *(Italy)*

SURFACINGS 3

"silence is so accurate"
— Mark Rothko

only the sound of rain that song falls silent
a lightbulb. turn on the radio
empty the ashtray of muscles flaunted
in the business of war of profits
breaking the steps the silence
at the bottom of the heart was babel was babylon
was fallen sky. you can ask the wind
was desert. was sunset
was empty western star over the burning city
something somebody. just glimmers
with face turned to the stars
water flows slow light
what do you want me to do with my words?
what am I supposed to write?
in gray landscapes with poisoned waters
rubble of cement skeletons
my eyes hurt. workers' stories
construction site collapse in Florence. then the screams
every number hides names and stories
the shameful ranking of the dead
soap bubbles
amid the racket of shitting money
poetry cannot. must not be silent
to chase the sun a shiver. prayer
hear the singing frogs
where can we go dancing. to warm up from the cold
write to me when you get home
I feed on your absence

tocco l'orlo della tua bocca
aperta alla libertà
sorride alle mie dita
che affondano. nella profondità
dei tuoi capell
un gesto largo le braccia
gli occhi fissi al cielo
e dentro tutto grida del subito guerra
nel marciapiede sconnesso
foglie parole
del se del forse del possibile
con urgenza. inaspettata
ed è subito ancora giorno
e lo stupore arde
a resistere
e scatto al rosso
volo salto
assetato

I touch the edge of your mouth
open to freedom
smiles at my fingers
that sink into the depth
of your hair
a wide gesture the arms
eyes fixed on the sky
and inside everything screams of war now
on the busted sidewalk
leaves words
of the self of maybe of the possible
with urgency unexpected
and suddenly again it's day
and the amazement blazes
to resist
and I dash at the red
fly leap
thirsty

(Translated from Italian by Lapo Guzzini)

LUÍS FILIPE SARMENTO *(Portugal)*

BELIEVE

Believe in God, the gods, the angels, the bouncers of heaven and hell; believe in popes, priests, imams, spirit guides, shamans; believe in the virgin and don't blush; believe in banks and bankers, governments and rulers, economists and kleptocrats; believe in doctors, hospitals, lawyers, courts, engineers, shipyards and the military; believe in the temples of manipulated food, in infinite consumption, in bank loans, in commerce and in trafficking; believe in the militancy of chartered ecologists, in NGOs, in public and private partnerships, believe in the incomes that allow you to live in misery; believe in the parlance of the unions of states, in weapons and bombs; believe in the education of uniforms, in the authoritarianism of all kinds of fascism in advanced, muscular and infamous democracies; believe in promises and waltzes, in the vomit of multinationals; believe in the intestinal gases you breathe every time world leaders open the terminal hole in the digestive tract; believe in the multiplied exclusivity of counterfeiting; believe that you know first-hand what is hidden from you in confiscation; believe in cancer teas, barbiturates, dreamless sleep; believe in social illusionists, instrumental pacts, employers' associations; believe in institutional unions and that madness is treated in hospitals; believe in everything, everything that saps your dignity and perhaps at the end of your life you'll realize that you've believed in everything except your own micro-happiness. And at that point, the mirror will just be a redundancy of your miserable life, leaving you only the lethal function of playing the final role of Santa Claus in the edenic patriarchal world. And the wind will be the contentment of your ashes without memory, without history, which will intoxicate those who breathe the dust of your belief.

Ladies and gentlemen, don't forget that you too can believe in the multicolored revolution of exaltation. Handmade. As handmade as your mental health. Go in the peace of Satan. Who, as you can see, doesn't even believe in himself.

JOANNA SCANDIFFIO

YOUNG WHITE MALE SHOOTERS

perhaps they weren't breastfed   maybe they didn't have religion
starched shirts on Sundays

maybe they forgot to carry the fifth commandment

or is it simply that they lived in a house with a picket fence
two parents and one dog

that mythical family where everyone hides from one another

maybe they played too many video games   were gluten intolerant
went off their meds   had a sugar rush   a bad day

a day when they didn't know how to say   they weren't Superman

a day they turned to the screen   watched a mass shooting
over and over like a really good movie

recognized themselves   a comrade-in-arms

while we were too busy with our Netflix series   our internet speed
to notice   they wanted us to notice

their skull and crossbones flag

maybe it was us   who forgot   to milk cows with them
when rust on the old barn door began to peel

when a shiver of fear ran up and down our spines   and
we thought
it was someone else’s kids and they were monsters

KURT SCHWEIGMAN

LEONARD PELTIER

Hang in there brother
freedom is on the precipice
a kicking and screaming America
has no choice but to change
toward diversity

Racists and those spreading hate
will always need someone to blame
for their own shortcomings
they were scared of
the American Indian Movement
all those decades ago
they're still making you burn
for their own sins

What more can I do?
bring the dynamite
for those cinder blocks
bring the acetylene torch
to cut those steel bars
bring sacred medicine
to humble your captors
into understanding
your innocence

The same blood
that runs through you
runs through me
our ancestors common
from a great tribe

Here I am still believing
the president will do right
pardon you to freedom
with your remaining time
to experience liberty
sacred ceremonies
hugs from your family
all the good
that you've missed

So I am here, still writing
continuing to educate
so others will understand
this grand injustice

As you suffer, sacrificing for us
Dakota and Lakota
Očhéthi Šakówiŋ (The 7 Council Fires)
and all indigenous people
while the establishment
their bellies continue to be full
with all the good cuts of meat
as we are continually thrown scraps
yet, becoming stronger each day
        rising up again
        and again
        fighting injustice
let them pick the bones out of that

NINA SERRANO

WHEN THE BANKS ARE FULL OF MONEY

When the banks are full of money
And the cupboard is bare
Things have to change
Things have to change!

KIM SHUCK

RAIN OVER TILLICUM

> *At night when the streets of your cities and villages are silent and you think them deserted, they will throng with the returning hosts that once filled them and still love this beautiful land. The White Man will never be alone.*
> *-Attributed to Chief Seattle*

Rain won't break until next Tuesday
So for now I will sit with you here
Watching the water in the
Sound the
Texture of my love for this place is the
Smell of fresh gathered
Mushrooms and almond candy
We are all mispronounced in all directions I have
Built poems to support my children and yours
Into the future
Some of us made it I have brought you a
Crabapple and some
Cold roast duck
Neither one of us myth
Yet

DINO SIOTIS *(Greece)*

ΣΚΕΛΕΤΟΙ ΣΤΗ ΝΤΟΥΛΑΠΑ

Σκελετούς στη ντουλάπα τους κρύβουν τα μέγαρα,
οι πρεσβείες, τα ανάκτορα, οι τράπεζες, οι μυστικές
υπηρεσίες, οι πολυεθνικές, τα κοινοβούλια και όλα τα

υπουργεία όλων των εθνών, οι σκελετοί στη ντουλάπα
ζωντανεύουν γύρω στα μεσάνυχτα όταν έχει πανσέληνο
και σαν μάγισσες ή σαν νεράιδες παίρνουν σβάρνα τις

χώρες και τις ηπείρους να πιουν λίγο απ' το αίμα των
φτωχών, των αδύναμων, των κατατρεγμένων και των
άμαχων, μ' αυτό το αίμα κρατιούνται ζωντανοί στη

ντουλάπα, μετά πάνε σε ένα wine bar στο κέντρο της
πόλης να θρηνήσουν το πληγωμένο τους γόητρο κι
όλα τα αμαρτήματα εξουσιαστών και εξουσιαζόμενων

DINO SIOTIS *(Greece)*

SKELETONS IN THE CLOSET

Mansions and palaces and banks and the secret services
and the multinational companies and the parliaments and
all the ministries of all nations are hiding skeletons in their

closets, the skeletons come alive around midnight when
there is a full moon and like witches or like fairies they
harrow in countries and continents to drink some of the

blood of the working class, the weak, the downtrodden
and the homeless, the skeletons with this blood they are
kept alive in their closets, then they go to a wine bar in

the center of it city to mourn their injured prestige, to
drown their tight misery in a discomfort survival, to
wash off them all the sins of the rulers and the ruled

(Translated from Greek by the author)

DOREEN STOCK

THE PRAYERS AT AMIZMIZ

These are the prayers for the dead
uttered by those left to stand in their place
in the shocked void shattered beyond
their understanding

And so they stand in an open space
a small road leading off behind
into the unknowable tomorrow as today
is unknowable, yesterday, unknowable
unthinkable, so many of them leaving in an instant…

“I can’t bear that my child should see this many
dead,” wept one man, coming at last to stand
here with his fellow creatures, clothes on their
backs, yes, heads covered by a gaping sky above
feet clenching an unsteady crust below. They gather
just beyond what once was their Amizmiz, now their ruin
to question the eternal, to bless whom they have lost,
to plead with the eternal, to weep to the eternal, to
join themselves back into an unfamiliar world, to
pray for sustenance, that the throbbing silence
cease, and the tolling in their ears of the cries of the
doomed.

Amizmiz, Morroco, September, 2023

MATTHEW TALEBI

RED WASHED HOSPITAL SCENE

Screams
Wounds
Dusty faces
Sanguine smell
Despair and fear

Surgeon cutting, sewing lives
too busy all night
to give his son a call
wishing him a good night

Early next morning
the grave morning,
Here Dr.
Nurse rushed a pale body in her arms.
Here Dr.
"Oh boy, oh boy,"
Doc murmured
Running his hand over the boy's forehead
I am here ma'dear
The boy's hazel eyes gazing at him
Half smiled
Father saw the thin smile
before the eyes and lips both froze
His life just the last moments
Or was it a dream?
Mute tragedy scarred Dr's heart
"Our son is gone, forever "
Sun also disappeared.
Day and soul darkened.

SARAH THILYKOU *(Greece)*

ONE

Two mothers
Hagar and Sarah
the bond
the free one

Two sons
Ismael and Isaac
the son of the bond
the son of the free

Yet
"there is neither bond nor free"

Two pairs of warm brown eyes
expelled
in the desert of the world, where
"the scorpions of the earth have power"

Two sons, Abraham's
fighting
for love
for tolerance
as the sun sets in a hungry sky
bleeding from crimson to purple

Two sons
two suns in the sky -
One God
reigning over that very sky

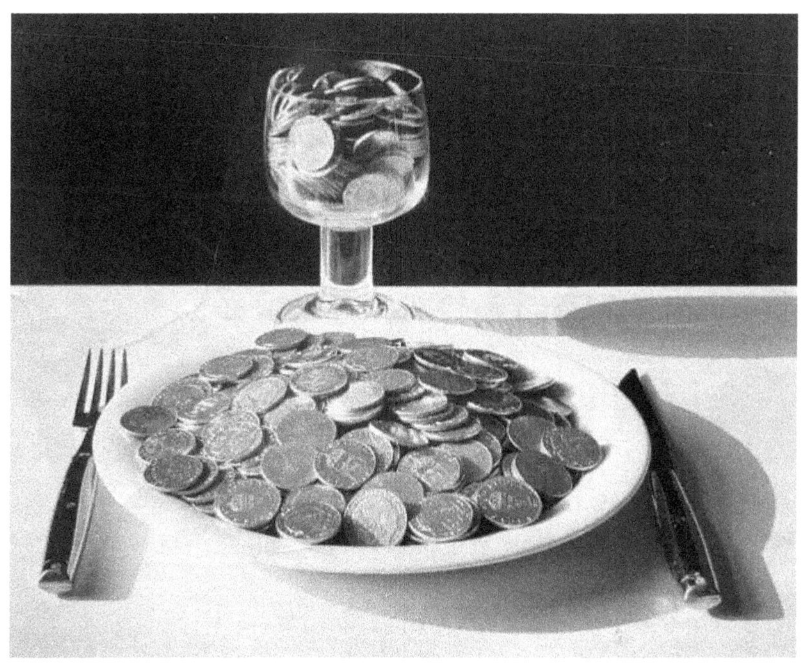

Horst Tuuloskorpi

RAYMOND NAT TURNER

WAR CRIMINAL BASSACKWARDS TRIBE

Not now, nor have I ever been a
Member of remote-controlled,
Battery-operated, black bourgeois
Judas Quisling skin folk stratum ...

Not now, nor have I ever been a
Member of the black bourgeoisie's
Strong-arm Williams- Thom-ass
Clarence-led Bassackwards Tribe ...

Got 0 love for Bassackwards Tribe militantly
Toasting—drunkenly saluting— Atomic Aunt
Jemima blowing up every anguished UN plea
for Ceasefire!

0 love for Bassackwards Tribe shrieking
Wildly for Raytheon's Raven, flapping
White phosphorus wings over
Our planet, cawing, "War forever more!"

0 love for Bassackwards Tribe celebrating
Bought and bossed Capitalist Hill
House Negroz—schlepping skunk
Water for apartheid state gangsters

0 love for Bassackwards Tribe praising the
Press secretary checking boxes—
Bombing homes, hospitals and schools—
Glamorizing genocide for an embalmed boss

O love for Bassackwards Tribe at war with us
Lunch bucket, gloved, steel toe booted-brothas/sistars.
At war with us of box-stacking, truck-loading; floor-
mopping-toilet-scrubbing tribe

O love for Bassackwards Tribe at war with us un-
varnished, us rough-hewn
Resisters! At war with us unruly midwives of the
World where we ***can*** breathe ...

BHISMA UPRETI / भीष्म उप्रेती *(Nepal)*

म

म छु
तर म मात्र छैनँ ।

चराहरू छन् र उनीहरूको चिरिबिरी सङ्गीत छ
जनावरहरू छन् र उनीहरूको गतिविधि छ
हिमालहरू, हिउँहरू र बगिरहेका नदीहरू छन्
रुखहरू, फूलहरू र बहिरहेका सुगन्धहरू छन्
अरू पनि धेरै छन् मान्छेहरू
र इर्ष्या, द्वेष अनि प्रेम पनि छ सँगसँगै
जीवनबाट नछुट्टिने
सपनाका रङहरू छन्
ती हल्लन्छन्, फर्फराउँछन्, उड्छन् र तैरिन्छन्
अक्षर, शब्द र अर्थहरू बन्छन् ।

मैले आफू मात्र सोच्नु भनेको
सृष्टिको विरुद्ध हो
म जाबो केही रहन्नँ
यी सबैबाट अलग्गिएर ।

म छु
तर म मात्र छैनँ ।

BHISMA UPRETI *(Nepal)*

I

I am there;
but I am not the only one that exists.

There are birds; their sweet ditty resounds,
there are beasts; their movement rustles,
there are mountains, and on them are piles of snow
wherefrom, rivers emanate
there are trees, fruits and the fragrance that flows,
there also are other people
and with them are their avarice, hatred and love,
there are hues of dreams
that never snap their ties with life;
they sway, flap, fly and float
and take shape as letters, words and meanings.

For me, it's against the code of creation
to think only about myself;
Set apart from all these
I will be of no worth.

I am there;
but I am not the only one that exists.

(Translated from Nepali by Mahesh Paudyal)

VIVIMARIE VANDERPOORTEN *(Sri Lanka)*

VACANCY FOR A HANGMAN

Wanted, a Hangman.

Attributes: Moral fortitude
Strength of Character.

Nature of Duties:
Pulling black hood over irony
Executing convicts
 accurately
Tightening rope around
righteous anger

Preference will be given to someone who is:
Able to shut trapdoor to

            his conscience

Deaf so he cannot hear his heart
            scream
            Blind so he cannot
            see himself
            become
            what
            he
            kills.

DAVID VOLPENDESTA

FORBIDDEN PSALM TO FINDING PEACE THROUGH THE IMAGINATION

To Everyone

Because the imagination is real,
peace is a fragrant rose
blooming in your hands.
In a field of lilies,
children show adults how to dream
far beyond infinity.
Peace is a caterpillar
climbing an oak tree
whose leaves are orange and red as the sun.
Yes, peace is a forest
where roses bloom,
squirrels and foxes play,
and the caterpillar becomes a monarch butterfly
soaring into the bright morning light.

DIANE WARD

WOMBWORTH

How many new soldiers can you provide for men?

We don't discriminate too much.

Send us your sons and daughters.

We don't discriminate, too much

Soldier up, soldier down, we don't mind your periodic menses too much, anymore.

An ability to fight and take direction, silent sighing, whimpering from all the genders, don't care too much anymore.

How many new soldiers can you provide for men?

Most with wombs would rather bargain, perhaps, don't assume for that would be a mistake.

Womb holders can be just as treacherous, ego vampires sucking their juices from wherever they can...so just remember and let's get to the point

How many new soldiers can you provide for men?

Almost sounds like a choice, right?

Tired of what seems like busywork, new patterns of 'put-off and wait some more" crafts, listening through their faulty ear, postponing unnatural deaths you accelerate to help, and all the cookie cutters wombs can hold just as long as you can birth soldiers provided for men.

While you are commerce-d for your labor rarely tallied, you have no time to dally, You soldier up, soldier down, fields, canneries, sweatshops, grain-ery. seashores, every nook and cranny for food sustenance, and the wheel of homespun, nameless in labors of both types, basketed awaiting your loin-dropped expecting to full suckle on your exhausted frame,

new soldiers for men.

Apparently, some men were not crystalized first in wombs, but raised forfeiting others their opportunities to rise in equality.

Apparently, politics frame some mothers' hips

Determining what's best for her nation's future is the additional labor role placing both she and her babies at risk

Poking in any fertile field, men don't discriminate if it's soldiers they need.

Muted by the blasts, their wives and daughters safely set aside. Teaching them to raise only those bred to order and profit somehow in all the ways war benefits are designed. Blast and rebuild, wound and become a hospital guild, war has benefits mortar, plaster backroom cast, heatseeking drones drop food, medicines and possibly blaster sealing caps.

The personhood with those who provide the blood and guts of the marginalized only good enough to strut flags and leave their teeth, return if "lucky?" less a spleen, bury their bone parts in lands where men of war surf.

"Almost terribly sorry" for your loss, but you're still young, "bear-able" and have ample, nice, full beauty spots. So, tell me, how many new soldiers can you provide for men?

Gather data, quantify, keep you busy, commute, commune and smile. Can I sit at the big table yet, please? Stilettos, falsettos, comfortable pumps have no place in the damming deal. We can entertain calmly and compromise at the sanity not vanity table.

Work and work and scan the globe, have you enhance your segregated title, labeled and staffed roles, and carry on, fearlessly charting the woes of women. Womb holders labor pains otherwise forgotten and build and concretize what men of war all too well already know, who still believe a pat on the head is sufficient setback for our political power accountability, and enforcement needs woes.

Since we're talking, while you're here how many soldiers can you provide for the war's needs? So, noted.

MICHAEL WARR

TO YOUR ASSAILANT – WHO ATTACKS US ALL

Do you call yourself God-fearing?
Devoted to "do on to others"?
Does your God condone your violence?
Your ignorance?
Your corruption?
Does your God hate your neighbor?
Like you do?
Does your God share your love
For Prophets bearing "false witness"
Fueling your grievance fever?
Do you swallow the lies they regurgitate?
Do you really need a reason?
Are you truly a True Believer
of both God and Golden Calf?
Does the All-Knowing know you?
Do They love you as you are?
Does it matter that They are watching
Your naked depravity?
Do you pray before you prey?
On innocents in this guilty world?
Do you have your God's blessing?
Or are you as Godless as you seem?
Did your father teach you
to beat, demean, and maim?
Is he proud of your cowardice?
Does your mother say "well-done son"?
Did they train you in backwardness?
Do you feel bigger in your smallness?
Content with acts of uselessness?
Is your inner bully seething still

beneath your concealed surface?
Are you comforted in your criminality?
Stupefied by “superiority”?
Simply insane? Or lost?
Who are you?

CATHLEEN WILLIAMS

FOR ALL

the light upon the sea
silver upon gray

for all
the low moon orange
at midnight

for all
love
for the barely loveable

for all
quiet presence
responsibility

the birds lifting
way out free

for all

NELLIE WONG

...WORDS ARE POOR THINGS

—Marilynne Robinson

Poor things. Lying
on the street, on Polk and Willow, hungry for touch.
In flight longing for embrace
Oh yes such earthly creatures
lean, curled in arms, tent dwellers
sharing day-old bread, eyes open, blink
in light of dawn
Dogs bark at passers-by tapping
their cane, wheeling, moving on
Poor things. Mannequins wearing
sequin-spangled dress, silver-lame tights,
posing behind shuttered store window
annoying silence
Cater-corner essence, odiferous
and free, tipsy without bars
Things. Things.
Material to live by, labor of bodies
of words imprisoned
'til fingers unlock language,
attention to deed.

LORENE ZAROU-ZOUZOUNIS *(Palestine/USA)*

BETRAYAL

While the extreme form of capitalism consumes precious
seconds,
minute by minute, hour by hour,
ingesting days and nights until one loses count,
loses oneself.

The Homo erectus, us, who roam a wretched earth;
us, larger-than-life-personality dinosaurs
in search of water, oil, gas and blood-
flirt with cannibalism and laughing sinisterly at genocide.

Cruel creatures, us humans, once opulent and mighty
in simple ways, in wholesome ways-
the lucky ones, gifted at birth with a heart, a brain,
and perfectly designed limbs.

We learned nippily to squander nature's generous
marvels-
trading in our own hearts and souls at the neighborhood
pawn shop,
for money, objects, status, power and control.

It is not the mighty and exquisite earth that is wretched,
Indeed, it is the opposite,
for the Earth Mother is patient with evil.
It is the spineless human, the sadistic one that is vile,
wretched.
I leave many out of my tirade. I love you!
Peacemakers and lovers of justice,
be assured your heart and soul is not in jeopardy.

Your work in this realm is not complete.

To immoral humans who murder 95 babies each day,
lie about it with propaganda for complicit killers to repeat.
To despicable humans who drop illegal white
phosphorous,
setting aflame precious bodies from the inside out,
I say, go back to hell where you came from,
take a number, wait in line, beg to purchase
a heart and a conscience. You have the money!
You will know then, the joy of what true humanity feels
like-
with a new heart and human conscience.

To depraved humans who drop 2000-lb U.S.-made bombs
on innocents, dance on graves and steal bodies,
commit targeted assassinations with tested AI apps-
I say, go straight to hell where you come from,
take a number, be seated next to murderous comrades.

To depraved humans who sing while scooping up
massacred,
mutilated bodies with U.S.-made bulldozers, hide them to
prevent a count or a proper burial;
all see how a starved entrapped indigenous population is
treated-
entombed in a concentration camp, with no exits-a killing
field!
I say, go to where you know your heart coexists,
ask nicely for a new heart as this will be a redemption.

To those vile ones, who continue, for 7 decades to steal
land,

shred all that is life-sustaining away from a bombed-out
people,
besiege a country for 17 years, by land, air and sea,
leaving a beautiful people and culture to eat grass and
fodder-
you know the drill by now, that many a peacemaker has
spelled out.

Planet earth's gifts that gives life,
sustains life, now more than ever, has taketh us all
asunder;
Among pitying and giving resilient trees, sun and sky,
watching us fail,
attempting to save us by offering fallen fruit and rain.

Years and decades pass and more are swallowed whole,
chomped by the extreme form of capitalism,
The Military-Industrial-Complex and its greedy dragons.
The money count is imperative. Keep churning,
turning the economy, digging holes for graves,
building more weapons, digging more 6' holes.

The moment of truth is a shooting star only seen
by an innocent child who has yet to be wolfed down by
a system.
With each lunar and solar eclipse,
dwindling cold cash dissolves like space junk,
hurled about in winds of a Pentagon budget,
yet again, increased and saved before a Congressional
recess.

Gobbled up personalities, devoured hearts,
lavishly nibbled on, spitting out more and more
sour, heartless jingoes-

souls unrecognizable for any
guardian angel or true-life angel to locate,
to save, to transform, to dissuade.
All the while as the elected seek dirty cash for their dirty
thoughts
and their sadistic deeds, in a republic hijacked for the
elites.

While The-Military-Industrial-Complex
is a religion of choice, coercion, or bribery,
abandoning the land of the three monotheistic religions is
betrayal!
Drop by drop licking and slurping up the downtrodden,
as if preparing for mummification
embalming while eyes shut,
is drying out evil souls in the process.

ANDRENA ZAWINSKI

SAN FRANCISCO TALE OF TWO CITIES

(found poem from Violet Blue's introduction
A Fish Has No Word For Water:
A Punk Homeless San Francisco Memoir)

San Francisco,
home to 75 billionaires
and 8000 homeless,
billionaires and millionaires
from Lyft, Stripe, Twitter
and more opposing taxes
to fund homeless shelters.

San Francisco,
a handful of diamonds
glimmering in the ebony palm
of an outstretched hand
under spires hemmed in
by water so dark it seems
to absorb light.

San Francisco,
a fog-softened grid
of streets melting down
over hills sliding to pool
in valleys where tech buildings
tower over block-long lines
for shelter beds.

San Francisco,
sky a chock-a-block of Victorians
and their gemstone streetlights

divided by noir shadows,
air punctuated by moaning
nighttime foghorns in the shade
of cyber punk towers.

San Francisco,
occult jewel glowing in tufts of fog
along dreamland paths of fault lines,
subterranean schooners paved over
for our futuristic skyline atop
marshland filled with refuse
and shifting sand dunes.

San Francisco,
whose homeless sleep in parks
circled by mansions and soaring
views of the Golden Gate,
starved in the dirt, fantastic
technologies fueling the heart
of a shining future—

San Francisco. San Francisco.

BIOGRAPHICAL NOTES

ADRIAN ARIAS is a poet, visual artist, and activist. He is the creator and curator of *Tarot in Pandemic and Revolution*, from Nomadic Press, 2022.

AYO AYOOLA-AMALE is a poet, artist, and Director of the Splendors of Dawn Poetry Foundation, in Nigeria. Her poems confront violence, racism, and the breakdown of the Yuma community.

MAHNAZ BADIHIAN, a poet and artist, has published many books in Farsi and English. Her recent collection of poems, *Ask the Wind*, was published by Vagabond in 2022. She runs, Mahmag.org.

LISBIT BAILEY 's most recent chapbook is *Horizon*. She co-edited the 2021 and 2022 RPB anthologies. Her poems are in This Wandering State, from caliballiance.org; *Tarot in the Time of Pandemic and Revolution* from Nomadic Press, and *Third Rail*'s online incarnation at literatureandarts.com/.

LYNNE BARNES is the author of *Falling into Flowers* (2017). Her work appears in *Poets11: Fog and Light: San Francisco through the Eyes of the Poets who Live Here and Light on the Walls of Life.*

VIRGINIA BARRETT is a poet, writer, artist, editor, and educator. Her six books of poetry include *Between Looking* (Finishing Line Press) and *Crossing Haight—San Francisco poems* (Jambu Press).

ALESSANDRA BAVA is an Italian poet and translator of the poem of Marco Cinque. She is writing a biography of SF Poet Laureate emeritus Jack Hirschman.

BENGT BERG is a Swedish poet and activist who's published 40 books, mostly of poetry, which have been translated into many languages. He was a member of the Swedish Parliament from 2010-2014 representing the Left Party.

JUDITH AYN BERNHARD Is the author of the poetry collection, *Prisoners of Culture* and a book of short stories, *Marriages.* A former language instructor, her literary translations and poems have appeared in numerous anthologies. She lives in San Francisco and teaches writing.

DANIEL BROOKS is a writer, poet, editor, and special education teacher. His work has appeared in *Indianapolis Review, Hawai'i Review, People's Tribune,* and on Kallatumba Press

KRISTINA BROWN is a visual artist and writer, and a co editor of this anthology. She often writes about what people will, and will not, do for love. Having spent her childhood in Japan and Okinawa, she is an admirer of bokeh and the crack that lets the light in.

JANET CANNON is the author of three chapbooks: *Day Laborers, The Last Night in New York,* and *Percipience*.

YOLANDA CATZALCO is a Mexican American poet who lives in San Francisco. She advocates for the homeless, the undocumented immigrants, especially essential workers, and for addressing climate warming.

MARCO CINQUE writes, photographs, plays ethnic instruments, recites, publishes essays, poetry collections, and articles. He has published more than 30 books and has been translated into English, Spanish, Albanian, and French.

FRANCES COMBES is one of the most politically engaged poets in Paris and all of France. He is the coordinator of the World Poetry Movement for Europe, and the leader of a group of French poets, le Merle moqueur.

KITTY COSTELLO's collection *Upon Waking: New & Selected Poems 1977-2017* gathers 40 years of her San Francisco writings. She is co-editor of the anthology *Muslim American Writers at Home: Stories, Essays & Poems of Identity, Diversity & Belonging,* helping to overturn Islamophobia.

ANITA ODENA CRUZ is a member of Hayward's B Street Writers Collective and Bay Area Poets Coalition. She won first-place prizes for *Make a Living as a Poet* and *Edith,* and read at Jack Hirschman's Poets 11 for Bayview, SF.

ROMEO ALCALA CRUZ writes poetry in both English and Bicol (rawit dawit). He is the author of *Washing Rice and other Poems* and *Crossing the River from Memory to Forgetfulness.*

JOHN CURL is a co-editor of this anthology. His latest poetry collection is *Rainbow Weather: Poems for Environmental Healing* (Vagabond Books, 2022). He recorded his poetry for Voetica.com. His work can be found on www.johncurl.net

LUCILLE LANG DAY is the founder of Scarlet Tanager Books and a science and health educator. She has written or edited over 20 books and is a contributor to over 50 anthologies.

CAROL DENNEY is a Berkeley cartoonist, poet, and musician. An award-winning lyricist, poet, guitarist, fiddler and concertina stylist, she was a founder of "Fiddlers for Peace," curator of the "Deep Poetry Project," and founder and editor of the *Pepper Spray Times.*

GERMAIN DROOGENBROODT has written 17 poetry books, published in 31 countries. He has received many international awards, is yearly invited to international poetry festivals, and was nominated in 2017 for the Nobel Prize in Literature.

CARLOS RAÚL DUFFLAR is a poet, playwright, peace activist, and a member of the New York Revolutionary Poets Brigade. He is also a member of the Academy of American Poets and, as of

September 2023, a New Generation Lifetime Beat Poet Laureate.

AGNETA FALK Is a poet, artist, and a member of the World Poetry Movement. She is preparing her third major volume of poetry for publication.

MAURO FFORTISSIMO is an Argentinian/Italian/American musician, painter, poet, and activist. Born in 1962, he moved to the US and the Bay Area in 1980.

DAVID FLEISCHMAN. After retiring (from OEM factories) at age 70, I decided to use my natural tendency to seek off-beat paths to share ideas through creative writing. I have been published in my synagogue's bulletin and the Edgewater (Chicago) Library magazine *Writings From The Edge*.

MARCOS DE SOUSA FREITAS is a poet, engineer, and environmental and cultural activist. He lives in Brasilia and is the author of *In The Coming Afternoon.* He is the current president of the Academia de Letras do Brasil (ALB).

LUIS GARCÍA explores his ancestral roots through a myriad of visual and written artistic processes. There is a duality, a split in having been born into one culture (El Salvador) raised in another (U.S.), seen as immigrant, now as citizen. Dichotomy is a word that seems to best describe his arrival to this worldview, a worldview that has been in process his whole life.

RAFAEL JESÚS GONZÁLEZ, retired professor of Creative Writing & Literature and Mexican & Latin American Studies, was four times nominated for a Pushcart Prize, and was named the first Poet Laureate of Berkeley, California. Visit http://rjgonzalez.blogspot.com

ART GOODTIMES, poet, basket weaver, and former Green party elected official in Colorado, served as Western Slope Poet

Laureate and is currently poetry editor for fungimag.com and sagegreenjournal.org

EGON GÜNTHER lives as a poet and painter in Upper Bavaria.

SATISH GUPTA is an Indian painter, sculptor, poet, writer, graphic artist, muralist, designer and calligrapher. His illustrations adorn Germain Droogenbroodt's latest poetry collection, *The Road of Being*.

LAPO GUZZINI is a San Francisco-based translator, editor, and arts agitator. He has translated the poem of Sandro Sardella in this issue and is completing a book of Sardella's poetry.

KAREN HARVEY-TURNER is a Chicago-based poet, artist, guerilla gardener, and former children's librarian. She has published work in the People's Tribune and the Revolutionary Poets Brigade's anthology *Overcoming Capitalism: A World Without Wars*, and is a member of Chicago Poets United to End Homelessness.

BILL HATCH is the editor of Badlands Journal and works on environmental issues in the San Joaquin Valley. He is also author and composer of *Shellburg Blues*, and translator of poems of Roque Dalton.

MARTIN HICKEL, child of the paradise which is the San Francisco Bay region, has always wondered why more people don't open their eyes. He's been busy doing nothing and going nowhere for a while now and hopes to continue as long as possible.

JACK HIRSCHMAN, who completed his life work defending the planet and building socialism, was both an emeritus Poet Laureate of San Francisco and co-founder of the Revolutionary Poets Brigade.

EVERETT HOAGLAND lives in New Bedford, Massachusetts, has published five books, and his poetry has been published in The

Progressive, Political Affairs, The Workers Weekly World, Spare Change, and in anthologies *Resisting Arrest, Stand Our Ground, What Saves Us, Ghost Fishing: An Eco-Justice Poetry Anthology, Liberation Poetry*, and *Afro Asia.*

SUSU JEFFREY grew up in the American Midwest on mashed potatoes and politics. Her first two books were about her Roma (Gypsy) ancestry, followed by collections about politics, love, water (*Mississippi Mother*, spoken word CD) and now trees.

ZIBA KARBASSI, born in Tabriz, Iran, and living in the UK, is widely regarded as the leading Iranian poet living in exile. She has published over twelve volumes of poetry, been translated into over fifteen languages, and reviewed by numerous critics. She was chair of the Iranian Writers Association (in exile); chair of Exiled Writers Ink in UK; and a director of PEN International (Iran in exile) from 2019 to 2021.

ELIOT KATZ is the author of seven books of poetry, including *Love, War, Fire, Wind* and *Unlocking the Exits*, as well as *The Poetry and Politics of Allen Ginsberg.* He has worked for many years as an activist for peace and social-justice causes, including helping to create housing and food programs for homeless families in Central New Jersey. www.eliotkatzpoetry.com.

KUSAL DHANANJAYA KURUVITAGE studies Intention, Conservatism, and Thomism as student of faculty of law, Colombo university and Sri Lanka Law college.

D.L. LANG is an internationally published poet who served as poet laureate of Vallejo. Find her at poetryebook.com

JENNIFER LEONG (aka Soy Avocado) advocates for hope through her poetry, which is often multilingual and multidirectional, and believes in the power of the Word. She is active in both spoken and written word.

LI-MING LEONG. Singapore-based poet Li-Ming loves words whether written, spoken or sung. She hopes that all her written works let others experience the despair and the magic that lie beyond the everyday.

MARK LIPMAN, founder of Vagabond press, the Culver City Book Festival and the Elba Poetry Festival, is author of more than twelve books, including *The Role of the Revolutionary Poet in Society*. His radio program, Poetry from Around the World, is on KPFK 90.7FM Los Angeles. Mark is currently traveling the world, building consciousness through the spoken word.

OSCAR LOCATELLI lives in Bergamo, Italy, where he is a redactor of a magazine of workers' writings, *Abiti/Lavoro.* In the 1980s he was poet-editor of "abiti/lavoro" (clothes/work), a magazine of workers' writing. A trade unionist, he was mayor for 10 years of Paladina, his hometown.

ANNA LOMBARDO, poet, free translator and cultural activist, lives in Venice and is the art director of the International Poetry Festival Palabra en el Mundo. Her recent poetry books include *Con candide mani* (2020), *Con candidas manos* (2023), and *Blackout* (2024). Her poems have been translated into multiple languages and presented in national and international journals and anthologies. A guest in many international poetry festivals, she is among the founders of Poets of Planet (POP).

ZIGI LOWENBERG is a performance poet and co-leader of the jazzPoetry ensemble UpSurge! which has produced CDs under the name, *All Hands on Deck*.

KIRK LUMPKIN is a poet, performer, spoken word artist, lyricist, environmentalist, cultural worker, and event organizer. Author of two books of poetry, he lives in Mendocino with his wife on 80 acres of undeveloped land; his recent project is writing about poison oak.

BIPLAB MAJEE is a leading Bengali poet, writer, literary critic and translator. He has published 28 books of poetry, 36 books of prose, and 16 books of translation.

ELIZABETH MARINO is a Chicago-based RPB member, poet, educator, and performer. Her work has appeared in 20+ anthologies, as well as the full-length collection *Asylum* and two chapbooks.

ÁNGEL L. MARTÍNEZ is a poet, musician, peace activist, and a member of the New York City Revolutionary Poets Brigade. He plays bass guitar, guitar, and electronic effects.

CINDY A. MATTHEWS is the head writer of *The Revolution Continues* on Substack and a freelancer for a local alternative newspaper. She is also a published novelist and short story writer. Every once in a while she writes poetry.

TOMMI AVICOLLI MECCA is a queer, southern Italian/American poet whose work has appeared in newspapers, anthologies and journals since the late sixties.

KAREN MELANDER-MAGOON is published in many anthologies, has sung major opera roles in Europe for two decades, and has five CDs online and video of her *Lillie, A Musical*. She is an interfaith minister and a co-editor of this anthology.

SARAH MENEFEE is an activist for the poor and homeless. She was a founding member of the League of Revolutionaries for a New America, the Revolutionary Poets Brigade, Occupy SF and First They Came For The Homeless.

TUREEDA MIKELL is a story medicine woman, poet and Black Panther alum, committed to voices of the people. She has published over 70 at-risk student anthologies, featured nationally and internationally. Her recent book is *Synchronicity: Oracle of Sun Medicine,* by Nomadic Press 2020,

NANCY MOREJÓN is one of the finest poets of contemporary Cuba.She lives in Havana and often visits and reads in the USA and Europe.

EDWARD MYCUE, born in Niagara Falls NY, and lived and studied in TX, MA, UC Berkeley, Elsinore DK, and Legon GHANA. His first volume of poetry was *Damage Within The Community* (1973), more recently *Mindwalking,* and his first online book is *I Am A Fact Not A Fiction.*

MAJID NACIFY, considered the Arthur Rimbaud of Persian poetry, was born in Iran in 1952, published In *the Tiger's Skin* in Persian, fled Iran in 1983 after the execution of his wife Ezzat in Teheran, and received a doctorate in Near Eastern Language and Culture at UCLA.

JEFF NOWAK is a librarian from Chicago and abuses his work time by encouraging patrons to write and express themselves.

BARBARA PASCHKE, translator and musician, is a co-editor of this anthology. Her many multilanguage publications include *Volcan* (co-edited with Alejandro Murguia), *Clamor of Innocence,* and *First World Ha Ha Ha* (City Lights. She is a member of the SF Bach Choir and the Roque Dalton Cultural Brigade,

SERENA PICCOLI is an Italian poet and playwright. She writes both in Italian (her mother tongue) and in English mainly about social injustices. https://serenapiccoli.wixsite.com/serenapiccoli Interview in Tint Journal: https://tintjournal.com/interview/the-international-political-poet-an-interview-with-serena-piccoli

GREGORY POND, a prolific poet featured in many magazines and journals, currently hosts a poetry series at the CLARION Performing Arts Center in Chinatown, as well as organizing poetry sessions for the elderly. His work was recently featured in the Haight-Ashbury Literary Journal.

KATHY POWERS at the age of 50 realized her voice was the voice of the people, and became a revolutionary activist fighting to raise unheard voices. She lives in the Chicago area

THORWALD PROLL, born in Kassel, West-Germany 1941, became a militant member of the Students Movement, therefore spending two years in jail. He published his firstbook, while he was illegal. His latest book is *The Ideal World The Poet Of Passersby*, 2023.

MARGARET RANDALL is an American writer, photographer, activist and academic. Born in New York City, she lived in New Mexico and for many years in Spain, Mexico, and Cuba.

D. A. "ROARSHOCK" WILSON is a San Francisco poet, author of *First Hours of a Rainy Day and Other Poems,* and publisher of *Roarshock Page,* a literary street flier. He reads regularly, locally and internationally, in person and via the social web, and can be found online at his website. www.roarshock.net

LEW ROSENBAUM is a poet active both in the League of Revolutionaries for a New America and the Chicago Revolutionary Poets Brigade.

NICK SAMARAS' books include *Hands of the Saddlemaker* (Yale Unversity Press) and *American Psalm, World Psalm* (Ashland Poetry Press, 2014).

SANDRO SARDELLA is an Italian poet and painter who has done major exhibitions of his painting, featured also in this anthology.

LUIS FILIPE SARMENTO Portuguese poet, writer, and filmmaker. His many books and writings have been translated into numerous languages. His recent books include *40 Poemas 40 Pinturas: 40 Poems 40 Painting, The Intimacy of Sleep* (Water Mirror).

JOANNA SCANDIFFIO poet, educator and gemologist living in San Francisco. Her poems have been published in *Switched-on Gutenberg, Sugared Water.*

KURT SCHWEIGMAN was born and raised in South Dakota and is currently living in Sonoma County. He is an enrolled member of the Oglala Lakota Nation, a father, public health professional, poet/writer, and longtime advocate for the release of American Indian political prisoner Leonard Peltier. Kurt's forthcoming bilingual poetry book, *Roots Define the Reach of My Branches* (Gilgamesh Press), will be published in Mantua, Italy.

NINA SERRANO received the PEN award for *Heartstrong: selected poems* and the Best Book Award from Artists Embassy. She produces *Open Book* on KPFA-FM radio, and *La Raza Chronicles*, and was one of the founders of the Mission Cultural Center in San Francisco.

KIM SHUCK is the 7th Poet Laureate of San Francisco Emerita. Shuck's latest books are *Noodle, Rant, Tangent,* a collection of essays, *Pick a Garnet to Sleep In,* a collection of poems, and This *Wandering State vol. 2,* an anthology in a series of anthologies from specific areas around California.

DINOS SIOTIS was born in Tinos, Greece in 1944. He is editor of the literary magazines *(de)kata* and *Poetix*, runs the (de)kata publishing house, directs the Tinos International Literary Festival, and is currently president of the Greek Poets Circle.

DOREEN STOCK is a poet and activist, writer of *My Name is Y, a memoir of an anti-nuclear demonstrator*; she lives between Argentina and the SF Bay Area. Her other recent books are *A Noise In The Garden* (Kelsay Books, 2021), and *Your Excellency, Free Will* (translations of Amparo Casasbella Alconada, with Marcelo Holot), Prosa Amerian Editores, Argentina, 2021.

MATTHEW TALEBI is a poet who lives in the Los Angeles area. He immigrated to the United States from Iran in 1984. A retired ophthalmologist, he began writing socio-political poems in 2017.

SARAH THILYKOU is a Greek poet, translator, essayist, book reviewer, and editor. Her publications include *Duet of Islands* (Kyoto 2018), and *Angelic Flights* (New York 2021).

RAYMOND NAT TURNER is a NYC poet privileged to have read at the Harriet Tubman Centennial Symposium; he is artistic director of JazzPoetry Ensemble, UpSurge!NYC, which has appeared at numerous festivals and venues including the Monterey Jazz Festival and Panafest in Ghana, West Africa.

HORST TUULOSKORPI is a Swedish photographer, noted for his documentation of women's work at industries in Norrköping. His works have been published in many books beginning in the 1970s. He lives in Stockholm.

BHISMA UPRETI is a Nepali poet, essayist and novelist. His 22 books (9 volumes of poetry) have been translated into numerous languages. He has represented Nepal in many international literary conclaves. A Gold medalist of the Nepal National Poetry Festival, he is the recipient of SAARC Literature Award, Gopal Prasad Rimal Rastriya Kavya Puraskar, Uttam Shanti Puraskar, Yuva Varsha Moti Puraskar, Shankar Lamichhane Youth Essay Award and many more. Currently, he is secretary of PEN Nepal.

VIVIMARIE VANDERPOORTEN is Senior Lecturer at the Department of Language Studies, Open University of Sri Lanka. In addition to her own poem in this anthology, she is also the translator of the poem by Kusal Dhananjaya Kuruvitage.

DAVID VOLPENDESTA is a member of the Friends of Durruti, the Roque Dalton Cultural Brigade, and the San Francisco Revolutionary Poets Brigade. He is the author of *Forbidden Psalms* and is currently working on *Forbidden Psalms II.*

DIANE MURRAY WARD is a New Yorker of West Indian descent, whose works include modern dance choreography, blog talk, radio hosting, writing reviews, and performance poetry at many local and international venues, including the Nuyorican Poets Café. She is an active member of the National Writers Union.

MICHAEL WARR's books *include Of Poetry and Protest: From Emmett Till to Trayvon Martin* (W.W. Norton), *The Armageddon of Funk, We Are All The Black Boy*. In 2017 he was named a San Francisco Library Laureate.

CATHLEEN WILLIAMS is a Sacramento poet and editor of the newspaper Homeward. She is also a member of the San Francisco RPB.

NELLIE WONG is a Socialist feminist activist and author of several collections of her poetry. Editor of *Talking Back Voices of Color* (Red Letter Press), she dreams in jazz, bards in Hoisan American dialect, and cooks for working-class solidarity.

LORENE ZAROU-ZOUZOUNIS is a Palestinian-American writer and poet. She writes poetry for all ages, prose, historical fiction for children & adults, short stories and science fiction.

ANDRENA ZAWINSKY is a Pittsburg born working-class poet and photographer who lives in Alameda, California; she is recipient of the Oakland PEN Josephine Miles Prize for her poetry.
Her poems have received accolades for free verse, lyricism, spirituality, and social concern. Her latest and fourth full-length book of poetry is *Born Under the Influence* (2022 WordTech's Word Speak), a feminist and social activist collection.

REVOLUTIONARY POETS BRIGADE
MISSION STATEMENT

NOW
As poets we are uniquely positioned to seize the possibilities of the time, bringing language to life and participating in the movement that is gathering as we speak...

IT'S TIME
Poetry has always been and continues to be not only the way the poet listens to his or her innermost being, but a way the spirit of the times, in its most forward-looking incarnation, is expressed and heard. And the times we're in, of crisis and the cry for transformation, particularly needs the news, as poet W.C. Williams said, "without which we die."

We say what we see: and that is the system that cannot rest until it extracts every drop from a desperate earth: capitalism. We say what we see: and that is the oppression of our class, driven to the streets and alleys of our cities, driven to the muddy fields, all because there is no profit in maintaining life and health. We are the harbingers of revolution and the awareness that underlies and drives it.

FOR THE REVOLUTIONARY POETS
In our common struggle toward freedom, each individual instinctively reaches for the best tool at hand. As artists, we have the most powerful tool of all, the ability to inspire, transform, and liberate, just in the nick of time as it happens, as the sick old ways rust, choke, sputter, and fade. Poets, those at the compressed razor-sharp edge of social thought, and all fellow artists of visionary courage,

stay mindful of this historic opportunity, and lead with strong revolutionary voice for all humankind to genuinely live and thrive in common spirit!

BRIGADE
Therefore, we want to create a Revolutionary Poets Brigade, to respond to the demands of the moment – provoking the future out of the confused minds of today, inspiring with the passion of the living word, in preparation for the development on a wider and larger scale of the uprising, the action that will overthrow this system of greed and exploitation.

As a network, we can be present and participate in the popular resistance that is going on around us by holding poetry events, by reading and speaking at demonstrations, and by publishing broadsides and pamphlets. Join us.

"Camerados . . . will you come travel with us? Shall we stick by each other as long as we live?"
–Walt Whitman

REVOLUTIONARY POETS BRIGADE
http://revolutionarypoetsbrigade.org

www.ingramcontent.com/pod-product-compliance
Lightning Source LLC
LaVergne TN
LVHW050640100826
845148LV00011B/1926

* 9 7 8 0 9 3 8 3 9 2 1 8 7 *